Is It God or Am I Crazy?

My Unexpected Journey
Through Pain
to Happily Ever After

By
Lynn Severn Blankenship

Published by
The Digital Word Publishing LLC

PRAISE FOR
IS IT GOD OR AM I CRAZY?

"This book is more than a story of someone's life. It is a declaration that God is with us even when circumstances are completely contrary to what we thought or believed they should be. I know that this book will be an encouragement to all who read it, especially those going through difficult times. Lynn writes with openness and honesty, sharing her story in a way that encourages us that God desires to walk with us and lead us through life's circumstances."

> Maureen Woodcock
> Minister of Pastoral Care
> Genesis Church, Bloomington, Indiana

"This moving memoir tells the story of a young woman who doesn't want to be a pastor's wife. She listens to God's voice as she dates one young man in her teens, but eventually marries another, a pastor, and walks reluctantly into a role she has resisted, learning to trust God's voice in her journey. As she gains peace in her role, Lynn hears yet again a strong whisper that gently gives her the devastating message that her husband will die young, that she will be widow. Over a period of years, Lynn questions—yet believes—this whisper, as she awaits its fulfillment. She is assured that it will be in the fullness of time, and that God will provide for her, as he did for Ruth, land and a Boaz. Lynn's authentic, poignant story will touch its readers and inspire each to listen well for God's loving whisper."

> Dr. Holly Allen
> Director of Child and Family Studies Program
> and Professor of Biblical Studies
> John Brown University

Is It God Or Am I Crazy?

"The reader can feel God's whisper throughout this powerful journey of Lynn's life. We see the thread of a faithful God leading her through each chapter of her life as Lynn shares her heart on paper with us. The beauty is in the story she tells and the life she lives."
Jennifer Watson, Pastor's wife
Bella Vista Assembly of God

"Every follower of Christ struggles from time to time with hearing God's voice. Yet hearing his voice and doing what he says is essential to following him. Is It God or Am I Crazy? is the story of how Lynn Severn Blankenship learned to recognize his voice and trust him even when his still small voice shared a message she did not want to hear. This is a truly amazing story filled with unexpected twists, surprising confessions, tragic outcomes and victorious endings. Is It God or Am I Crazy? Is filled with life lessons for church planters and those who love them!"
Steve Pike
National Director of Church Multiplication Network

"This is a memoir that will hold your interest all the way through. The story moves forward with a steady and exciting pace and makes a full circle to a very happy conclusion. It emphasizes that those who are faithful in their relationships with God and man will receive a great reward from life."
Professor Cornelius House
Department of English, Purdue Calumet University

Lynn Severn Blankenship

Is It God or Am I Crazy?
My Unexpected Journey Through Pain to Happily Ever After

Cover photo and author's portrait © 2010 DonyaFaith Photography
Used with permission

ISBN for Paperback:
13 digit 978-0-9860346-1-9
10 digit 0-9860346-1-4

Published by The Digital Word Publishing, LLC,
212 Hernando Rd., Winter Haven, FL 33884.
Your Partner in Christian Digital Publishing.

DEDICATION

This work is dedicated to my beloved in-laws, George and Carol Severn. Without the gift of their son, Rev. Jimmy Ray Severn, I would have no story to tell.

"I tell you the truth, unless a kernel of wheat is planted in the soil and dies, it remains alone. But its death will produce many new kernels—a plentiful harvest of new lives." John 12:24 (NLT)

The scope of the harvest has yet to be perceived.

I also wish to honor my late father Bill Richardson, my mother Joy Richardson, and my brother Rev. Bill Richardson for living out the character of Christ in front of me and teaching me, even as a child, to always be listening for God's faintest whisper.

An affectionate thank you goes to my loving and supportive husband Rev. Dr. James R. Blankenship for motivating me to put pen to paper and share my miraculous, God-given story with others.

While the story that lies beyond may seem an improbable tale, it is completely true. Only a few inconsequential details and names have been changed to protect the privacy of some and to keep the book a reasonable length.

TABLE OF CONTENTS

CHAPTER ONE

THE PORCH

It is a peaceful scene in the early fall of 2012. There is crispness to the cool morning air – a welcome change from the unusually hot, dry summer that preceded it. The early morning sun moves slowly across vibrant orange and yellow leaves causing them to sparkle against the leaves still green beneath them.

A middle-aged woman sits rocking on the front porch of her brand new home in the country. An aging cat she calls Noah lies curled up in her lap. She can hear the faintest prrrrrrr as she gently stokes his soft, black and brown tabby head. Every now and then he gently nuzzles her arm with his wet, pink nose. He has been her faithful companion these past thirteen uncertain years as they have been through many changes together. Time and change have made him more than a mere pet to her.

He is a thread that connects the life she used to know with the one she knows today.

She is surrounded by the tranquility of untouched, rolling pasture-lands, and the woods that lie beyond. The slow-paced grazing of cattle is interrupted only by the sudden movement of two young calves skipping playfully on their way to the pond for a drink. She picks up a steaming cup of freshly brewed coffee with her left hand and slowly takes a sip. "A-h-h-h-h-h-h," she says with delight as she lays the cup back on the table beside her. She loves her morning coffee.

In her right hand she clasps the hand of her sweetheart sitting in the rocking chair next to her. He is keenly aware of her presence, but his attention is captured by the intrigue of the dusty old book he holds in his other hand.

She turns her attention away from Noah and the grazing cattle just long enough to give her sweetheart an affectionate smile. She often turns and smiles at him when she knows he isn't looking. It is a simple smile of gratitude that he is there beside her. He is unaware of the single tear that has left her eye and is making its way down her cheek. It is a tear of joy, not of sorrow. She is overwhelmed with gratitude for the life God has granted her today and amazed by the journey that brought her here…to her new front porch.

As she smiles at him, her mind returns to a day over two years ago in early spring 2010. It was the day he introduced her to his students and colleagues at the University. She remembers how proudly he seemed to show her off that day and how happy she was to be on his arm. The day had felt much like this one. The air was cool but the sun shone so brightly it gave the impression that the air outside was warmer than it really was.

It was a Friday afternoon and her sweetheart's freshman Bible students were eager for class to begin. Not only were they curious about their prof's new love interest, but Friday was story time with Dr. B – a time when her sweetheart shared stories from his extraordinary life.

Dr. B had been referred to as the school's most intriguing prof by a number of his students and described as "a legend" by others. His array of life experiences and out-of-the-ordinary lifestyle had earned him those titles.

Dr. B had been a bachelor 49 years of his life. He had spent almost half of those years in school. In fact, he had attended five undergrad and graduate schools in five different states, earning three graduate degrees along the way. He'd had a myriad of jobs, everything from lifeguard to lawyer, and martial arts instructor to Greek language professor. His personal and professional travels had taken him around the world. He had travelled to countries as diverse as Belize and Indonesia and had taken advantage of teaching opportunities in the Philippines, New Zealand, and Austria. He had even taken part in an archaeological dig in Jordan.

Dr. B's living arrangements had been as diverse as his life experiences. His first move was from a peaceful home in the country to a rowdy dorm on a secular university campus. After a stint as a lawyer in the suburbs of Nashville, he moved east where he lived in one of America's oldest historic homes near Boston. His next move took him to an apartment in a ghetto near West Philly. But his most unusual accommodation was a monastery where he lived for a year and a half while attending graduate school. He credits his time there for inspiring his semi-monastic lifestyle.

Dr. B's stories about his life had intriguing titles and details. They were stories like "The Knife Wielding Maniac," "Monks or Hell's Angels?" and "The Time I Almost Accidentally Started a Cult." He had shared stories about dodging bullets, narrowly surviving a tumble off a treacherous mountain cliff, and serving papers to a murder suspect. He had served those papers on his way to dinner with a date. As he exited the car he told the young lady he was with, "If you hear gunshots, I'm probably the one getting shot at. So don't wait on me. Drive to safety and call the police!"

Dr. B's atypical life, as well as stories he'd shared from his past, had inspired a few unfounded rumors among his students. Evidence of this came one Friday afternoon as story time with Dr. B was about to commence. A female student raised her hand with an unlikely request. "Tell us about the mafia."

Dr. B quizzically peered over the black-rimmed reading glasses that sat on the tip of his nose and inquired, "Now why do you think I would know anything about the mafia?"

The girl slowly and sheepishly asked, "Weren't…you…*in*…the mafia?"

"If I said yes, would you believe me?" Dr. B responded.

Just as slowly and sheepishly the girl responded, "P-r-r-ob-ably."

Dr. B snickered.

Another student inquired of one of Dr. B's co-workers, "Is he the blind, Jewish guy who doesn't believe in God?"

In actuality, Dr. B was neither a Jew nor an atheist, nor was he a current or former member of the mafia. And although he had been plagued by some rather serious vision issues, he certainly wasn't blind.

Dr. B had set forth just a couple of guidelines for story time. First, students had to ask for a story. If they asked, he would oblige. Second, if he was in the story, the students could be sure it was true.

But on this particular Friday, this group of students was interested in only one story. You see, Dr. B, a bachelor of nearly 50 years, had just announced his engagement. When asked why a contented, 49-year-old, self-proclaimed bachelor and boycotter of relationships would trade in his solitude for marriage, he smiled slyly as he shrugged his shoulders and said, "I figure, if marriage makes me unhappy, at least I've had a good run."

Dr. B's romantic interest had sparked an intense curiosity among the students and faculty who knew him. The school was abuzz that first day Dr. B was seen walking across campus holding his sweetheart's hand. The episode had spawned all sorts of gossip, snickering, and even a few rumors that had to be put to rest.

One of Dr. B's colleagues shared an amusing dialogue that took place in his class that day. "Hey, who was that girl Dr. B was walking around holding hands with?" one student asked. The professor assured the class, "That's no girl. She's at least 18." Actually, "that girl" was a woman in her 40's, but she did have a particularly youthful look, especially from a distance.

When another colleague asked her class if they had met Dr. B's fiancé one student piped up and said, "Yeah and she's normal," as though he were surprised.

Some students seemed to think the couple an unlikely pair. If you had seen them together that day, you might have thought the same. Dr. B's sweetheart was quite into fashion and had taken great pains to maintain a youthful and stylish appearance. She had chosen her look carefully that day. She wanted to blend in with the college crowd and yet create an ensemble that was dressy enough to be taken seriously by the other professionals she would be meeting.

She chose her outfit from the ground up. Short, dark red boots, tailored jeans with a wide leather belt, a fitted black turtleneck and a short, ivory knit sweater that tied above the waist. She completed the ensemble with silver and red jewelry, a ruby red purse with black leather trim, and a silver heart clasp. She made sure every detail was just right.

Dr. B, on the other hand, had a stereotypical, professorial look. His appearance was more scholarly than hip. He was tall with a distinguished, handsome face and had a strong, square jaw. His hair and beard were silver, and he wore a pair of black-rimmed reading glasses that sat on the tip of his nose. His clothing hung loose rather than fitted, and his shirt collar lacked the crisp creases that would come from a fresh pressing. His choice of footwear for every occasion except the most formal was a pair of black sneakers – a juxtaposition of styles with that of his sweetheart, no doubt. But they looked happy together, and most everyone joined in that happiness when they were engaged.

Class begins. It's time for a story. Dr. B waits for the request.

"Hey Dr. B, how did you two meet?"

"Well, the fun story is, she picked me up outside my college dorm when she was 15 years old…" That was how his story began.

The sound of tires rolling onto the gravel drive draws the woman out of her sweetheart's class at the University and back onto her new front porch. She peers through a patch of trees and spies a red pick-up making its way up the hill. She watches as the truck rounds the curve past a large oak tree at the top of the drive and parks in front of the red barn that stands next to the house. It's George and Carol – a second set of parents to the woman whose own father passed away 11 years ago and whose mother lives three states away. They've come to celebrate the move into the new house. The aroma of fresh coffee and warm baked cinnamon rolls is ready to greet them.

George is dressed in his usual overalls and white t-shirt. Only today, he is sporting his "good" overalls – the ones kept back for special occasions. They are pressed and still dark blue - not yet faded by many washings or showing signs of hard work on the farm. Carol is dressed in a pair of black jeans and a blue, lightweight sweater. Her hair has turned white, but she dons a stylish haircut and her tan face still has a youthful glow.

They step onto the driveway and begin making their way toward the house. As George and Carol near her front door a new flood of memories is unleashed. In an instant the journey that had taken her from the cradle to this place played like a movie in the woman's mind. It began so many years ago, yet every scene of her life had been leading her from childhood to the serenity she now enjoys from her new front porch. Each step had been guided by a whisper – the whisper of a God who loves her.

Some call her journey a fairy tale. Others call it a journey of strange and wondrous coincidence. But I, the one who knows her journey best, the one who has lived the journey, call it a story written by God. So pull up a rocking chair, and I will share my journey with you from my new front porch.

CHAPTER TWO

AT HOME WITH JESUS

My journey begins in the late 1960's when I was just a small child - at home - with Jesus. This is where I learned that communication with God could be both profound and customary. This is where I learned to live life in his presence and be ever attuned to his whisper.

You see, in our home Jesus was not some distant being who lived far away in Heaven. He was a member of our family, who although unseen, lived with us and was well aware of every facet of our lives. We were taught to be careful what we said because, "Jesus is listening." We were taught to treat each other with respect because, "Jesus is watching." And when our hearts were broken we were always reassured, "Jesus is here to hold you." Jesus lived right there with us, always observing, always loving.

I remember my mother praying out loud as she went about her daily chores. She would talk to Jesus as though she could see him standing right before her in the room. Her heart was full of love for her Lord, and it often overflowed in songs of worship and prayer even as she swept the floors, folded the laundry, or rustled dinner onto the table.

In our home each day began with Bible study and prayer. That's because both my father and mother took seriously the counsel of Proverbs 8:17. "I love them that love me; and those that seek me early shall find me." (NIV)

One day during Bible study, my mother shared with me a scripture passage describing God as our Father. I couldn't wait for Dad to get home from work so I could share my new insight with him. My preschool mind, however, was a bit confused. As soon as Dad walked inside the front door, he was greeted with a very enthusiastic, "Hey! You're not my daddy!"

He grinned curiously and asked, "What?"

"You're not my daddy! God is!" I answered him with excitement, quite proud of my newfound wisdom.

My mother, looking a bit startled and yet amused at the same time, quickly explained that Dad was my *earthly* father and God was my *Heavenly* Father. I'm not quite sure how, but it seemed to make sense to me, even at the age of four or five.

On the weekends Dad would take his turn leading family prayer and Bible study. My brother, Billy, and I would act out Bible stories as Dad read them aloud. It was a kind of Bible charades, but instead of the audience trying to guess what the words were as they were acted out, the verses were read aloud first. Then Billy and I scrambled to act out the story before Dad moved on in the text. We especially enjoyed stories like Noah's Ark and Daniel in the Lion's Den that included animals because they were the most fun to portray. This was not a game Dad had intended us to play, and I'm sure he found it quite distracting. However, he was a kind and patient man, and I suppose he thought if we acted out the passage, we would be more likely to remember it later. At any rate, it kept family prayer and Bible study more interesting for us kids.

My parents were diligent about ending each day as it had begun. Either Mom or Dad would read and pray with us just before they tucked us into bed and turned out the lights. For some reason I remember this

Mom, Lynn, Dad, Billy – Sometime in the early 1970's

ritual with Dad more so than with Mom. Dad often read to me from a children's Bible storybook, a gift to me from my Granny. It held my attention because it was illustrated, and the pictures made the stories come alive. Other times Dad would read a short, yet carefully chosen passage directly from the Bible. On those occasions I requested a special passage, he was always willing to oblige. After reading, he prayed with me, kissed me on the forehead, tucked the covers snugly around me, and then without fail signed off with, "Good night. Sleep tight," just before he switched off the light.

Despite the influence of kind and patient parents, I could be strong-willed at times. That may come as a surprise to those who have known me only as an adult. But when your only sibling is a brother six years older, you learn to be at least a little assertive at times. My brother never roughhoused with me. And he could be quite protective if his little sister needed defending. But like most big brothers, Billy could be quite antagonizing and seemed to take pleasure in pestering me into a tizzy. It took only seconds of his pestering before I would tear into him kicking, screaming and scratching. I once became so angry with him that I threw a baby buggy wheel at Billy and broke off part of his front tooth. I'm sure

9

I claimed self-defense at the time, but that may not have been entirely accurate.

However, Mom was determined that her strong-willed little daughter was going to grow up to be lady-like and sweet, and she had her own unique way of training me to be just that. When Mom decided my temper had gotten the best of me, she would put her hands on her hips, peer sternly at me and ask, "Lynn, have you prayed today?"

"No!" I would often retort with a sarcastic tone.

"You go to your room and ask Jesus to help you calm down and make you sweet," she would say. "And don't come out of your room until your attitude has changed."

I was tenacious, but I did respect my parents. So I obeyed Mom's instructions, albeit in a huff. I marched to my room and closed the door firmly behind me. I would then spend the next few minutes sulking before kneeling by my bed. But when the sulking was over I would kneel down, ask Jesus to help me calm down and to forgive me for the anger I had just unleashed on my brother. I can't say I really expected any divine assistance as I begrudgingly huffed through my prayer. But much to my surprise, what started out as a reluctant prayer actually seemed to have an effect. I always emerged from my room feeling better and less like throwing baby buggy parts at my big brother.

Living with the awareness of God's presence allowed me to grow up with a sense of serenity I fear few children know today. Our home wasn't perfect, but for me it was a place of refuge, and the presence of God made it so.

Inviting God's presence to reside in our home did not exempt us from real life or its perils, however. My mother was visited by grief when her brother passed away at the age of 37. She had already lost one brother, struck by a car at the age of seven. Another pain would tear my heart when her parents divorced after 34 years of marriage. Their breakup would introduce a whole new set of stressful family issues.

Financial stress was a constant companion. My father also felt the weight of responsibility for his aging, widowed mother. Widowed in her 40's, she never remarried, never learned to drive, and never held down a full-time job. Making sure Mammaw's needs were met was a constant concern for Dad and demanded a great deal of his time.

However, when our family was faced with perplexing circumstances, there was no question what our first course of action would be. We would gather as a family and pray. Jesus was not only a member of our family; he was the resident advisor. This meant we consulted him about everything. After consulting him, we waited for the whisper of his still, small voice to provide the counsel we so needed.

I remember quite vividly getting just a little irritated when I would go to my parents asking for answers or advice on an issue. They would give me the same answer time and time again, "Just pray about it." It wasn't their desire to withhold constructive parental guidance, which they also offered. Rather, their admonition to pray about every situation came from their desire that I cultivate my own relationship with God, to learn to discern his whisper for myself. Part of helping my brother and me cultivate our own relationship with God was making sure we were in church every time the doors were open.

Our church was old fashioned in at least one sense. At the end of many a service we were invited by the pastor to come to the altar and pray. This was particularly true of Sunday night services. As an adolescent I thought this was an activity only for adults, and as soon as the call was given, I shot out the back door to the lobby to socialize with my friends.

Mom had no qualms with my social activities, but she wanted to instill within me a certain set of priorities. She instructed me one Sunday night that I was no longer to leave the sanctuary to socialize until I had taken at least a few minutes to pray. It annoyed me, in a way, but I complied and tried to spend at least a few minutes talking to God each time the opportunity was given.

Those times of prayer at the altar turned out to be most valuable for me. My usual prayer was for God's guidance in my life. I prayed that he would direct the decisions and events of my life, and that I would ultimately fulfill his will and purpose for me. It was during those times that I began to really listen for his whisper – that still small voice that says, "This is the way. Walk in it."

Is It God Or Am I Crazy?

As a child I could not fathom the consequence of my parents' lessons to listen for God's whisper. But I would stay in God's Word, I would pray, and I would listen as they had taught me. As I matured, I learned to recognize God's whisper as I made important life decisions. However, as important as hearing God's whisper would be for me as a young adult, it would be decades before I realized just how all-consuming and life-altering just one whisper from God could be.

CHAPTER THREE

HEARTBROKEN

I am most grateful for being raised by devout Christian parents who shared a heart for service. Working in our local church was a family affair, and provided opportunities to grow closer as a family while at the same time serving others. My father taught the adult Sunday school class and served on the church board. My mother had a heart for and worked tirelessly with Missionettes, a sort of Boy and Girl Scouts for church kids.

Mom and Dad loved reaching out to children and were committed to making sure any child who wanted to be in church had a means of getting there. They started giving neighborhood children rides to church in their four-door sedan, but it soon proved to be too small. My Granny heard of their dilemma and lent them an old station wagon that at least doubled their capacity to take children to church. When the station wagon proved to be inadequate, the church agreed to purchase a van. The route then expanded past our own neighborhood to the greater Bloomington area and occasionally onto the Indiana University (IU) campus.

It was the first Wednesday night in September 1981. I had just turned 15. Like every other Wednesday night our family was making their usual rounds to pick up would-be churchgoers. I always sat in the front between Mom and Dad. There was a large plastic console between the front bucket seats. It provided just enough space for one person to sit facing the back. This was my reserved seat.

Dad made his last stop outside Eigenmann Hall where we were to pick up a new IU student who had transferred in from Michigan State. The door slid open and a tall, tan, athletic young man hopped in. He sat in the middle of the first row, directly facing me. I would soon learn his name was Jim, but everyone called him Jimbo.

Later that evening Mom told me the first thing that popped into her head when Jimbo climbed aboard was, "Now there's a guy for Lynn!" I remember thinking he was kind of cute, but I didn't care for his brown suede shoes. I supposed the guy was nice enough, but when you're 15, something as trite as brown suede shoes can be a deal breaker. Besides, he had a serious look about him. I just wasn't interested.

A year passed. In that time Jimbo had completed his junior year at IU, gone home for the summer and returned to Bloomington to complete his senior year. I distinctly remember standing in the church lobby the first Sunday he returned from summer break. I looked over and saw him standing on the opposite side of the room conversing with some fellow students.

Had I not been aware I was in a public setting, I'm not sure I could have veiled my sudden fascination. There he stood, six feet tall, muscular and tanned, having worked outdoors all summer. He was wearing a dark suit, quite in style for the time. Now, instead of being focused on his brown suede shoes, I found myself beguiled by his rugged good looks and dark brown eyes. Although those brown suede shoes had kept this from being a case of love-at-*first*-sight, this second glance had reeled me in and left me hoping my mother was right. Perhaps this *was* the guy for me.

My parents had taught me well. So rather than go after Jimbo on my own, I did what they had always taught me to do. I prayed about it. I bombarded Heaven for divine assistance in getting Jimbo's attention. At age 16, I knew a college senior with his sights on law school was really out of my league. Getting a date with this guy would take divine intervention.

I did have a few things going for me, however. To begin with, Jimbo and I had both been raised in conservative Christian homes. Both of us were serious about our relationship with Christ and were faithfully committed to being a contributing part of our local church. We both had a desire to please Christ and placed him at the center of our lives. This provided us with a common foundation. Secondly, my parents were impressed with Jimbo. Although he was several years older than me, they viewed him as a gentleman and someone who could be trusted with their daughter. Jimbo and I were the same ages my parents were when they started dating, and both our mothers had married spouses several years older than they when they were only 17. Consequently, the difference in our ages didn't seem to be an issue for my parents. Should Jimbo ask me out, I had their full support.

Jimbo and I were both active members of the youth group. At each function I endeavored to build a rapport with him and offered him my friendship. This kind of effort was out of character for me. Although I had been a boisterous child, I had developed a quiet, timid nature as a young teen. My timid nature often made cultivating new friendships a struggle. There was something about Jimbo that made me feel at ease though, and my hope that we would end up as a couple made it worth the effort.

Our youth group would often go out for pizza after Sunday or Wednesday night services, and Jimbo graciously offered to drive me home since I didn't have a car. This provided a convenient opportunity to get better acquainted. Those trips home were marked with easy, pleasant conversation, and we both seemed to enjoy our time together. I hoped and prayed they would continue.

Jimbo seemed happy to call me his friend but reluctant to pursue anything more. I, on the other hand, was eager to call him my beau. As the first semester of his senior year was coming to a close, I thought perhaps I saw a small glimmer of hope. It was during rehearsal for the church Christmas program. I was sitting in the choir loft, and Jimbo was sitting on the platform steps waiting for his cue. The pastor's wife had asked me to cast the drama that year, and I had cast Jimbo as one of the three Wise Men. We caught one another's eyes and gave each other an affectionate smile. Our gaze stayed fixed just long enough to reveal each other's interest before needing to refocus on our portion of the program. Could a date be just around the corner?

It was January 1983 now, and Jimbo had started his final semester at IU. Despite any interest he may have had in dating me, he still had not asked me out. I knew if there were any chance of dating him, something had to change and change quickly.

One of Jimbo's buddies from home was also attending IU this particular year. Kent and Jimbo often came to church together, and I had become friends with Kent as well. I figured if Jimbo had any feelings for me, Kent would be the most likely to know it. I also suspected he was the only person who might manage to light a fire under Jimbo to ask me for a date.

One Wednesday night before youth service commenced I sat down in the chair on Kent's right. Jimbo sat on his left. I leaned over to Kent and whispered, "Does he have a girlfriend?"

"Not that I know of," Kent replied.

I responded, "He probably doesn't want one, does he?" Jimbo was serious about his studies, and it would not have surprised me to learn he had intentionally steered away from dating to avoid unnecessary distraction.

"I don't think anything's stopping him," Kent said. The conversation was left at that.

Kent must have taken my cue and had the talk with Jimbo I had hoped he would. Not a week passed before Jimbo asked me out for our first date.

I was elated. I had prayed, even begged God for this and my prayers had been answered.

Jimbo and I started spending as much time together as our schedules allowed. Sunday and Wednesday evenings after church were spent with the youth group at McDonald's or the local pizza joint. We almost always went out on Friday and Saturday nights and then came back to my parents' house until the strict 11:00 curfew my parents had set rolled around.

I think it pleased my parents that Jimbo was willing to spend so much time in our home. We would sit in the family room for hours and watch television with my parents until they decided to say goodnight. After they had gone to bed, Jimbo and I were allowed to enjoy a little "alone" time.

Mom had her way of making sure our "alone" time never got out of hand, though. It usually wasn't more than 15 or 20 minutes after she and Dad said goodnight that I would hear her call down from upstairs, "Lynn, would you fix me a glass of warm milk?" She said it helped her fall asleep, but I suspect the motive behind her request was more protective than medicinal.

My parents' bedroom was located directly above the family room. Mom must have been delighted with the architect, because his design had given her a perfect vantage point from which to monitor her daughter's dates. She would simply put her ear to the heat vent on the bedroom floor. From there she could hear everything being said in the room below. That is, until the heater kicked on and she was met with a blast of hot air. But Jimbo never gave my parents any cause to doubt his honor. He was always a gentleman and never once attempted to take advantage of his younger girlfriend. I loved and respected that about him. He always made me feel safe.

Jimbo was not one to carelessly bandy empty expressions of love and devotion. Neither was he backward about verbalizing genuine feelings of affection, whether in public or in private. In one particular youth service, we were asked to say something we admired about the person sitting to our right. Jimbo and I were at the end of the line and it was his turn to say something about me. I waited with anticipation to hear what he would say. "I can't think of anything I *don't* like about Lynn," he answered. I thought it a clever response, and at that moment I believe it was even sincere.

I recall another evening, this one at my parents' house. I remember the moment well. Jimbo and I sat in our usual spot, an oversized chair that was positioned in the corner opposite the television. We were both younger and leaner then, and both fit in the chair comfortably, albeit cozily. My parents had retired for the evening, giving Jimbo and me a little time alone. I'm sure Mom had her ear to the heat vent as usual, but we were given the sense of being alone, nonetheless.

Jimbo sat with his left arm around my shoulder, his right hand and my left hand clasped. "I think I love you," he said softly. I felt both joy and panic. I was speechless to respond at first. I wanted him to be in love with me, but not just yet.

My affection for Jimbo was growing, and I hoped we would marry someday. Although we hadn't dated long, I had spent enough time with him before we dated to recognize how special he was. He demonstrated so many of the qualities I desired in the one with whom I would spend the rest of my life. He was handsome but not vain. He was quiet but not coy, intellectual but not condescending. He was ambitious but well grounded, with a sense for keeping work and play in balance. He was affectionate but respectful. He made me feel loved.

But my desire to marry Jimbo went beyond his qualities and my attraction to them. It also stemmed from the fear of something from which I knew he could protect me – life in full-time ministry. I had often joked with my friends of my fear that God would call me to marry a short, fat, bald-headed missionary to Africa where I would be forced to live out my days in a grass hut.

Although I never really thought God would call me to a foreign mission field, there was a fear he would call me to be a minister's wife. I had come from a long line of ministers and was, at least in part, aware of the toll pastoring could take on a minister and his family. My grandfather, a pastor, had died of a heart attack at the age of 49. I had heard stories from my Mammaw of how hard Grandpa worked. At the time he died, he was not only pastoring full-time, he was working as a carpenter during the day and working on a new church facility in the evenings. The stress was simply too much, and in my mind, it was the demands of ministry that had claimed my grandfather's life. I had no desire to live my grandmother's life, and no desire to be a widow in my 40's.

Mammaw's stories as well as personal observations had made me aware of how difficult life in the parsonage could be. Parishioners could be harsh. Perhaps they were simply unaware of or just didn't care about how deeply their words and actions cut their pastors' hearts. Some felt it not only their right, but also their duty to make sure the pastor and his family conformed to their own set of preferences and expectations. If they did not see compliance, they would simply vote the pastor out or make life so unbearable he would be forced to resign. I didn't want to live in that kind of fish bowl and I certainly didn't want to raise children in it. That was my perception at age 16.

Time and experience have softened my perceptions and allowed me to see a softer, more positive side of ministry. But as a teen, I was focused on the negative. I was close enough to ministry to be frightened by it, and did not want to marry into its distinct hardships.

It was not that I had an aversion to ministry. In fact, I loved people and derived a great sense of fulfillment when given the opportunity to encourage others and point them to Christ, especially through music. I had plans to attend Central Bible College (CBC) to study voice and piano, as I aspired to direct a church music program. But I wanted to do it as a layperson, not as a pastor's wife. I thought if I went to Bible college as a single girl, I would end up married to a minister, and that thought frightened me.

I knew Jimbo had no aspirations for occupational ministry, although he himself had also come from a long line of pastors and missionaries. Marrying a man bent on a law career seemed a safe and simple solution. It would allow me to be actively involved in music ministry without the stress of being married to the minister. Also the security of a lawyer's income would allow me to offer my services free of charge should we find ourselves attending a smaller, less affluent church. It seemed like a win/

win situation to me. I couldn't imagine why God wouldn't be eager to endorse my plan.

I even had the timeline figured out. If I were willing to just get a diploma instead of a degree, I could finish college in three years. Since I already had plans to graduate high school a semester early and proceed straight to college, I could complete my education just one semester after Jimbo graduated law school.

It was my timeline that gave me pause when Jimbo said he thought he loved me. I feared if our relationship became serious too quickly, Jimbo would grow impatient while I "grew up" and move on to other romantic interests. I wanted our relationship to progress slowly and steadily over time, so that by the time we had completed our education, we would both be ready for marriage.

I often asked for God's counsel and guidance in regard to our relationship. Actually it was more asking God to work out my plan than it was about opening my heart to his. My prayers were more a plea for God to help me write my story rather than asking how he wanted to write me into his. I had it all figured out, or so I thought.

Then came the whisper. It's the first time I can remember hearing God's still, small voice. I was in my bedroom primping, as all girls do before an important occasion. Jimbo and I were going out that evening, and he was on his way to pick me up. I was styling my hair and making sure my make-up was applied just so. As I looked into the mirror, I heard a voice inside my head. "I'm letting you date him, but you're to marry another."

I was startled by the voice. It wasn't audible, but it might as well have been. It was just as though someone had sneaked up behind me and whispered, "Boo," in my ear. The voice, however, bypassed my ear and spoke directly into my mind and heart. I had a sense this was God's voice, but I despised the message and tried to dismiss it. My plan for my life felt comfortable and safe, and I didn't want God interfering with it.

From that point forward, I saw changes in Jimbo. He became more distant. The frequency of our times together hadn't lessened, but it seemed his affection for me had. I think the difference in our ages was becoming more obvious and more of a concern to him even though I looked and acted older than many girls my age. But looking older and knowing how to behave in social situations are no substitute for the growth and emotional maturity that come with age and experience. His reservations about a long-term relationship became apparent.

I remember a particular spring afternoon. I believe it was in late March, a little over two months since we started dating. It was unusually warm for the season, and Jimbo and I had driven to a nearby state park to enjoy a picnic with Kent and his girlfriend. Kentucky Fried Chicken and mashed potatoes were on the menu.

After lunch, Jimbo and I went up into one of the lookout towers. I'm not really sure what conversation led to his statement, but I distinctly remember Jimbo saying to me, "You're gonna make a great pastor's wife someday." I'm sure I looked insulted. I resented the remark; it made me angry.

"I don't wanna be a pastor's wife!" I snapped back.

I could see Jimbo's affection for me was waning, but I held onto the hope that I could gain back what had been lost.

The last few weeks before his graduation, I began to struggle with a series of what I would call mixed messages from Jimbo. One evening before church, Jimbo and I stood against a wall in the back of the sanctuary. A gentleman spoke to us as he passed on the way to his seat. "You two make a great couple," he said.

"Not for long," Jimbo replied, somewhat under his breath. One might consider the comment an obvious indication of his intent to terminate our relationship. However, other comments led me to believe Jimbo still had feelings for me and viewed us as a couple.

For instance, sometime in late April, our church sponsored a banquet for both high school and college graduates. Since Jimbo would be graduating that May, we attended the banquet together. Everyone was encouraged to take a few minutes to mingle before the program began. A young man, a dear friend since early childhood, approached me. As he held out his hand to shake mine, he looked up at Jimbo and asked, "Is it okay if I greet her?"

"Greet and *merely* greet," Jimbo replied with a grin. He seemed proud to have me on his arm, and his response to my friend was his light-hearted way of letting my friend know I was there as *his* date.

I wasn't sure how to interpret these conflicting messages. On the one hand, it seemed he was losing interest. On the other hand, it seemed he still considered us a couple and continued spending time with me.

One evening when Jimbo brought me home from a bowling date, I confronted him before we got out of the car. "You're getting tired of me, aren't you?" I asked.

With his hand gently stoking the back of my neck, he looked into my eyes, shook his head and said, "No. Not at all." Then he gave me a quick kiss goodnight and walked me to the door.

It was obvious Jimbo's feelings toward me had cooled. But at 16, I was naïve enough to believe our relationship was still going to work. I had seen the future I wanted, wrapped it up in a neat little package and was not about to let it go. I was in complete denial. If there was only a thread of hope, I was going to grasp that thread and hang on for dear life.

Graduation day for Jimbo finally came. Even though I had dreaded this day since we started dating, I was proud of him and happy to be asked to join his family for the ceremony.

IU had close to 40,000 students, so each school graduated several hundred at a time. As I took my seat in the stands of IU's Assembly Hall, I looked out onto a sea of black caps and gowns. Jimbo had attached a flag atop his cap so we could pick him out of the sea of graduates. I spotted him quickly.

After the ceremony I went to dinner with Jimbo's family. Then, it was the dreaded ride back to my house. The day of our parting had finally come.

"Let her down easy, son," Jimbo's father had advised him.

The problem was he let me down so easily I didn't realize I had been let down at all, at least in a permanent sense.

Our parting and the next several months following were full of mixed messages which continued to perplex me. That last day before he drove away there were reassuring hugs and kisses mixed with less reassuring comments. "It's going to be a little harder to set up dates now," he said. In my mind this only meant dates would be less frequent, not that they would cease.

"I'm still going to hear from you though, right?" I asked.

"I answer letters," he responded. And he did.

As best as I recall, Jimbo corresponded faithfully with me for nearly a year. But his letters were cold and impersonal. He didn't start them with "Dear..." and he didn't sign off with "Love..." I convinced myself it was because he just wasn't the mushy type. Even though deep down I knew, I couldn't bring myself to admit any chance for a future with Jimbo had passed.

I would later learn from someone who knew him well, the reason his letters were so impersonal, is that he saw no future for us as a couple and he didn't want to "lead me on," as it were. I suppose in his own way he was trying to protect me from false hope, but at the time I thought any communication was a reason for hope.

Summer came and summer went, as did my last semester of high school. I would graduate in December 1983 and start my first semester at Central Bible College (CBC) in Springfield, Missouri in January 1984. I had chosen CBC early on, possibly as early as my freshman year of high school. My father had spent two years there, and my brother Billy had graduated from CBC two years earlier. Billy's time there had given me a chance to see the school up close and become familiar with its small campus. I had visited the school twice during their "College Days" and felt very at home there. I was excited about this new adventure.

Dad was unable to take off work the week I left for CBC. It was one of his busiest times, and he was left with no choice but to stay behind and earn the living that would provide for my education. It made me sad to leave him behind. We were so very close. Yet I understood the nature of his work and understood that he would be coming with me if it were at all possible.

The day of my departure arrived. It was a cold but sunny day full of excitement and optimism. I loaded up the trunk of my brother's car with the few belongings I had. Then Mom, Billy and I took to the road and headed for Springfield, Missouri. We had always enjoyed traveling as a family, and this time was no different, except for the void we felt in Dad's absence.

We arrived at CBC about eight hours later. I quickly found my room assignment and retrieved my key. I had brought little with me, so unloading was quick. The dorm was new, and I found the room fresh and neat. It was more than adequate, and I was pleased with my new home away from home.

Mom and Billy wanted to get an early start the next morning, as it was a full day's drive back home. I remember the moment they said their good-byes. I was terribly excited to be there and eager to get the semester started. But I was still very young, having just turned 17. By all rights, I should still have been in high school, but an early graduation had allowed me to start CBC a semester early. A sense of insecurity and loneliness took hold of me. I remember my remark to them as they started to leave.

"You're just gonna leave me here," I said to them with uncertain, droopy eyes.

It was not a plea to go back with them, nor was it a request that they stay. It was simply a statement birthed out of a sense of being totally alone. I was timid and struggled with new friendships, and I worried how long it would take to find acceptance. I was already missing those I was leaving behind, and this new sense of isolation just served to intensify the aching that lingered from my parting with Jimbo.

I know my statement must have torn them up inside. They hated to leave me as much as I hated to see them go. But we were all confident I was where God wanted me, and he was not going to leave me just because I had a new address. Of that I was certain.

As I waved good-bye and started on the last bit of unpacking, I found a letter from my father. He had hidden it away where it would not be found until I was left alone. He was a man of few words, but they were full of love and wisdom, and I always sat at attention when he spoke. It read simply:

"Dear Lynn,

We are proud of you, and especially proud of your dedication to God. Remember that God is always first, and He will take care of us when we make Him first. Have a wonderful semester and remember we are praying for you.

Love, Dad

Proverbs 23:23-25 23 Buy the truth and do not sell it—wisdom, instruction and insight as well. 24 The father of a righteous child has great joy; a man who fathers a wise son rejoices in him. 25 May your father and mother rejoice; may she who gave you birth be joyful!"

How unaware I was of how significant the wisdom of that 23rd verse would become in my life! "Buy the truth and do not sell it – wisdom, instruction and insight as well." How unaware I was that there would come a time decades later, when God-given insight would collide with my peace of mind and all hell would break loose until I had the firmest handle on what was truth. The wisdom and instruction I had received as a child are what I would cling to as I endured the assault of that storm.

The transition to college may not have been as easy as it could have been had I been an older, more confident student. But all in all it was smooth. I soon found people ready to take me under their wing. My first semester, albeit a little lonely, was off to a great start.

As for Jimbo, we continued to write during my first weeks at college. But after nearly a year of dispassionate communiqués, I finally wrote to ask him just where I stood. I needed to know if he still cared about or had any feelings at all for me. I received this response:

"I thought you realized that when I graduated, our relationship would necessarily change...but in a sense, I do still care."

As much as I wanted to latch on to the words, "I do still care," I had to face reality. God was taking Jimbo and me on separate journeys.

We both knew I was too young to marry, and Jimbo was unwilling to maintain a long-distance relationship until I was ready. It was past time to let go.

I sent Jimbo one more letter. I told him not to expect future correspondence from me. I told him I could not move on to other relationships as long as I was in contact with him, because I would always be thinking of getting back together with him. The letter wasn't necessary, but it gave me a sense of closure I hadn't had to that point.

The ending of our relationship felt like a death to me, and I mourned it as such. Some say it is impossible for a 16- or 17-year old to know or understand true love. But the depth of pain I felt when I realized I had lost my Jimbo told me otherwise.

I wanted to believe that someday when I was older and we had both completed our education, life would bring us back together. But I knew in my heart the whisper I had heard over a year earlier was truly the whisper of God. He would grant my desire to date Jimbo, but as much as my heart ached to admit it, God's whisper was leading me down a different path – a path that did not include Jimbo. It was God's desire that I marry another.

The dissolution of my relationship with Jimbo would prove God's way of teaching me crucial lessons I would need to draw on later in life. I needed to learn to recognize God's whisper and respond to it without hesitation. I needed to learn a confidence in God my Father that would enable me to trust him through pain, a lesson that would one day carry me through an even greater pain.

CHAPTER FOUR

SAYING YES

With the matter of Jimbo behind me and settled, I was eager to know what future God did have planned for me. I was now open to exploring a new relationship, at least one with a fellow music major. I could see the wisdom in this. What a joy it could be to work alongside a husband who shared the same passion for music ministry. I could easily envision collaborating on large-scale musical productions – one of us accompanying, the other conducting. I could envision us composing music together and enjoying the satisfaction of hearing the music come to life as it was performed by a 50-voice choir. Yes, this had the potential of being a good, perhaps even preferable life to that of a lawyer's wife. I would keep my eye out for the perfect musician.

Is It God Or Am I Crazy?

Mornings at Central Bible College started with chapel. We were required to be in chapel five days a week and were allowed only a handful of absences each semester. Although it may have seemed a rigid requirement to some, I didn't really mind it at the time. This was simply a continuation of our family's custom of starting each morning with Bible study and prayer, and I found the exercise an uplifting way to start the day. It also facilitated a sense of personal growth as I endeavored to respond to the challenges from God's Word presented by the faculty and special guests each day.

During that first semester, though, there came a challenge I loathed hearing. It commenced in chapel, but it did not come from any speaker who was there that day. It was that whisper again – the same whisper I had heard tell me I was not going to marry Jimbo. The first time I had heard the whisper I questioned whether it was really the still, small voice of God. At the time, I was so convinced Jimbo and I would marry, I found it hard to believe God could be telling me otherwise. But it sounded like God's voice to me, and I remember thinking at the time, "If this really is the voice of God, and Jimbo and I don't marry, I will recognize it as God's voice the next time because I've heard it before."

I often compare recognizing God's voice to the way one recognizes the voice of a close friend or relative. The more time you spend with someone, the more familiar his or her voice becomes. And after a time, if they call you on the telephone, even though you cannot see their face, they need only say, "Hello," before you know who's on the line. You recognize their voice because you've heard it before.

The voice continued to speak as I returned to my dorm from chapel that day. I knew this was truly the whisper of God. I recognized it from before. He kept whispering to me, "You are withholding a part of your heart from me." I knew exactly what he was referring to and exactly what he wanted from me. But I did not want to relinquish my will, and a battle raged in my heart and my mind.

I had set my will against marrying into the ministry, at least ministry alongside a pastor. I had determined I would not even explore a relationship with a Bible major for fear I might end up married to a minister. Now God was asking me to say yes to that possibility.

I was familiar enough with stories from the Bible to know that those who sacrifice their own desires to embrace God's desires are eventually rewarded. Conversely, those who choose to rebel are inevitably worse off for it. In my mind saying yes to being a pastor's wife meant saying yes to a life of pain – a pain I was bent on avoiding. Now God was asking me to surrender to that life – a life that would require me to trust him through pain. The question was - did I trust God enough to say yes anyway.

I remember kneeling beside my bed after chapel that day. I even recall the prayer I prayed. "Oh God, I don't want to be a pastor's wife. But if that's your will for me, I'll do it." I felt more at peace, having submitted my will to Christ's. Yet in my heart and mind I desperately hoped God had only wanted my willingness, not my life. Only time would tell.

My third semester had now rolled around, and I was loving life. The whisper I had heard two semesters prior asking for complete surrender, had now moved to the back of my mind as I focused on more desirable adventures. The highlight for me was being part of Heart Song Choir. It provided an outlet for my greatest passion – sharing Jesus through music. Not only was I privileged to travel and perform in churches all across the nation, but the choir also recorded a number of albums and was featured on a weekly radio broadcast.

The choir was not only an exciting outlet for music ministry; it was also a great teaching tool. We had an outstanding director who knew how to inspire us toward both musical excellence and passionate, effective ministry. I learned more about touching hearts through music from him than I did in any classroom.

I remember a particular Heart Song service in which I was challenged not only by our director, but also by that whisper with which I was becoming so familiar. At the end of each service, either the director or a member of the choir would invite those in the audience to raise their hand if they wanted someone to pray with them. Members of the choir were encouraged to watch for those who desired personal ministry. Men would leave the platform and pray with men, and women with women.

I used to dread this part of the service. I loved singing, but I was timid and felt I lacked in the area of one-on-one ministry. I was nearly always the last one to leave the platform unless the director specifically asked me to leave sooner, and I never went to someone unless they had raised their hand asking for personal ministry.

On one particular Sunday morning in Indianapolis I noticed a young woman who looked to be in her mid to late 20's. She was sitting four or five rows back, close to the middle aisle with her husband. As the service neared the end, I found myself focused on her. I couldn't get her face out of my mind. Then I heard that whisper which was becoming more and more familiar to me. "Go to that woman." As reluctant as I was to go to anyone, even those who had raised their hand asking for personal ministry, I felt God was telling me to leave my place and go to her. I decided if she raised her hand, I would obey the voice and go. But when the audience was given the opportunity for special prayer, she did not raise her hand.

"Go to that woman," the voice prompted again.

I stood motionless on the riser, arguing with God in my mind. "God, I don't want to go to her. She didn't raise her hand. I don't want to embarrass her."

But the whisper was persistent. "Go to that woman."

After several minutes of arguing with God, I relented and went to the woman. I didn't know what else to say, so I simply told her I had felt God wanted me to come to her, and asked if there was anything I could pray with her about. She and her husband were gracious enough, but seemed hard-pressed to think of a prayer request. It seems they asked me to pray for God's blessing on the husband's business or some other job-related issue.

It seemed a pointless encounter to me, and I was unsure of why the whisper of God was so insistent that I go to that woman. But I had been obedient to his instruction and, as always, gained peace of mind knowing I had done what he asked.

As the men were tearing down equipment and loading the bus, I stood near the front of the church mingling and shaking hands. I noticed the woman I had gone to earlier walking toward me. She was alone.

"I've been waiting to talk to you alone," she said. "I wanted to thank you for coming over and praying with me. I couldn't say anything in front of my husband, but we've been having a terrible struggle in our marriage. I asked God, if he really cared to please send someone to pray with me."

Wow! I could not believe what I was hearing. I had heard of others being used by God in this way, but this was a new experience for me. I was so thankful God had chosen me to be the instrument of his love and reassurance for one of his hurting children. Not only did it give me an opportunity to bless someone in need, it gave me an opportunity to become even more familiar with God's whisper. He knew there would come a day when my recognition of his voice would be tested, and he wanted me to know it well.

Heart Song not only served to increase my ministry experience, it served to build self-confidence and opened the door to new friendships. Choir members stayed in church members' homes when we were on tour. Being forced to interact with total strangers from such diverse walks of life encouraged my social development, although I found the encouragement awkward at times. I enjoyed people and enjoyed social gatherings, but it was difficult for me to initiate conversation. I was more comfortable being reached out to than I was reaching out to others. I needed a trusted friend to help me connect with those I was meeting for the first time. I found such a friend in Debbie.

Debbie was another Indiana girl. She was attractive, outgoing, and seemingly adored by everybody. I think she must have noticed I needed someone to take me under his or her wing, because she did just that. She reached out to me during my first semester at CBC, and we remained the very best of friends. We ate together, traveled to Indiana and back together, and conspired together in our share of tour bus pranks.

One of those pranks still makes me chuckle. The choir had a long drive that day, and those of us who had not succumbed to slumber were overtaken by boredom. Debbie and I conspired to play a harmless prank on a fellow choir member. He sat sleeping with his head tilted back, mouth wide open, possibly even snoring. Debbie retrieved a tube of toothpaste and I proceeded to line his lips with it. We had just enough time to put the toothpaste back in its case before he awoke.

He didn't have a particularly well-developed sense of humor and was quick to voice his disapproval. "Debbie!" he barked.

"I didn't do it!" she snapped back.

I was not about to admit to anything. Since I was the one who had actually lined his lips with toothpaste, Debbie could honestly say she hadn't done it. And because of my mousey demeanor, I was rarely a suspect. As long as Debbie didn't have to take the rap, I figured what he didn't know wouldn't hurt him…or me.

Debbie would be graduating in May, though, and I dreaded saying good-bye. Her friendship over the past year and a half had meant the world to me, and I wondered who might fill her shoes as my dearest and most trusted friend. Little did I know that earlier in the semester God had already introduced me to my new best friend. It was an unlikely and quite accidental meeting. Although, looking back, I would say from God's perspective it was no accident at all.

I was signed up for Theology 2 that semester. It was the first day of class, and as I trekked across campus to my new classroom, I hoped all the way I would find someone there I knew. Starting a new class with a friend by my side always made the adventure a more pleasant one and made me feel less conspicuous in a classroom full of those more comfortable in new social situations than I was.

Fortunately for me, I spotted a former roommate sitting in the front row the minute I walked through the door. I was so happy to see her and immediately took the seat next to hers.

After I sat down, I looked over to see a young man I hadn't met before sitting to my right. He had thick, blonde hair and beautiful, steel blue eyes over which he wore a pair of metal-framed glasses. His skin was smooth, his cheeks were ruddy and he had a boyish look. He was a fairly short young man, no taller than five feet six or seven inches tall, and I guessed him to weigh at least 200 pounds, if not a little more.

For some reason the first thought that went through my mind when I saw him was, "I bet this guy never dates." I think it was more his expression than his appearance that led to my conclusion. He looked a bit bewildered, even a little sheepish. He looked so boyish and unsure of himself; I guess I just couldn't picture him mustering up the courage to actually ask a girl for a date. Looks, however, can be deceiving.

No sooner had the thought crossed my mind, that I heard that whisper again. This time it was as though God were standing in front of me, wagging his finger, shaking his head going, "Don't be so quick to jump to conclusions." As on prior occasions, I was startled by the voice.

The whisper took me back to a story I had heard from a guest speaker's wife who had visited my church months before. She told how she had met her husband at Bible school. She had not been attracted to or interested in him in the beginning. And just like me she was determined not to be a minister's wife. But her suitor had pursued her diligently, and after he had won her heart, they eventually married.

"God!" I said in my head, "you can*not* be telling me I'm going to marry this guy!"

This guy was obviously not what I was looking for. I had my heart set on a tall, dark-haired athletic type who could play the piano and sing. This guy was neither tall nor dark-headed, and since I hadn't seen him around the music school, I doubted that he was musical. He was obviously a Bible major, which to me was still taboo. Although I had told God I was willing to marry a minister, I was not enthused about teaming up with one. If God intended for me to marry this guy, he certainly had his work cut out.

I wasn't particularly rude to the young man, but I didn't go out of my way to get acquainted either. I ignored him as best I could for a time, but he made that somewhat of a challenge. For one thing, he would draw pictures on my notepad or scoot it about my desk as I endeavored to take lecture notes. His behavior was quite distracting but humorous at the same time.

I was accustomed to wearing flat shoes with no straps to class. I had a habit of taking my left foot completely out of its shoe and dangling the other shoe on the end of my right big toe. He liked to kick my abandoned shoe under the desk, making it awkward for me to retrieve. I found it annoying at first, but eventually it just became a silly little game we played. It was harmless enough, and I realized this was just his way of introducing me to his humorous side. I eventually found myself more amused than annoyed. He was actually kind of fun to be around. His name was Jim, but everyone called him Jimmy Ray.

Jimmy Ray was good for me. He and another classmate, Warren, invited me regularly to join them for lunch after Theo 2. Warren had aspirations of becoming a Christian comedian, and I had no doubt he would succeed. Jimmy Ray had a sense of humor all his own, and no doubt could have found success in the same field, but he was focused on more traditional avenues of ministry. These guys made me laugh, and lunch after Theo 2 became an anticipated highlight of my week.

Summer of 1985 quickly came and passed just as quickly. My fourth semester started with a bit of trepidation. I had many acquaintances, but no close friends – not the kind I felt comfortable enough with to drop by unannounced or to depend on to be a regular dining partner. I missed my buddy, Debbie. Her absence left me feeling as lonely as I had that first semester Mom and Billy dropped me off and waved good-bye.

When I went back to school that semester, I had traded in my specs for a new pair of contacts and had traded in my long, wavy Farrah Fawcett hairdo for a shorter, more stylish cut. The new look had boosted my confidence, but I still struggled socially.

The first or perhaps second day back, I was walking alone to the dining hall. I spied a couple I knew from Heart Song walking a few paces ahead of me. I picked up my pace so I could join them. I was relieved to see familiar faces.

"Hey, are you guys on your way to eat?" I asked.

The young man responded with, "Yeah, Lynn. But you know, now that Debbie's gone, you're gonna have to make a new friend. You can't just be a third wheel all the time."

I was a bit taken back by the comment. Perhaps he meant it in jest, but it made me feel unwelcomed at best. I ate dinner with the couple, but the young man's callous comment made me eager to leave and retreat to my room.

"Oh, God," I prayed, "it's so lonely here without Debbie. Please help me find a new friend."

A day or two later in the week, I saw Jimmy Ray and his roommate Dave walking across the courtyard toward me. I smiled and waved.

Dave smiled, waved back and announced to Jimmy Ray, "Hey, there's my friend, Lynn!"

Without a moment's hesitation, Jimmy Ray turned right back to him and declared, "She's gonna be more *my* friend than yours." He obviously approved of my new look.

Later that evening, I was feeling the need for a snack. The dining hall was closed for the evening, but the snack shop would be open until 10 p.m. So I took a break from studies and wandered down to the snack shop alone.

I ordered a bagel with cream cheese and topped off the order with a Dr. Pepper. "That should hold me over until breakfast," I thought.

I spied Jimmy Ray sitting at a nearby table, so I asked if I could join him. He and Warren had invited me to lunch so often the previous semester, I didn't think he would mind. I both hoped and suspected he would give me a warmer welcome than the two fellow choir members I had eaten with earlier in the week. He smiled politely and said, "Sure. Have a seat."

Jimmy Ray was a hospitable kind of guy. I think it was because he had been raised in a home where true, southern hospitality was a way of life. The door was always open, and as soon as you stepped through it, you were family. There was no pretense about him. He was who he was, and he made you feel it was okay to be whoever you were when you were with him.

We sat and talked about our past summer activities. I told him about my tour with Heart Song, and was surprised to learn he had spent his summer touring with Spiritwind. Spiritwind was another school-sponsored music group that consisted of a small vocal ensemble and a jazz band. Jimmy Ray was their bass guitarist. I would find out later, he was actually quite accomplished. It surprised me to find out how passionate he was about music. It seemed we had something in common.

I noticed some scraps of white paper lying on the table. Jimmy Ray picked them up and started creating origami. I quickly joined him. I don't remember the exact shapes his pieces took, but I remember being surprised by his creativity. He obviously had an artistic side to him. It was a pleasant, relaxed evening, and I was happy to join him again if and when the opportunity arose. As I walked back to my dorm, I felt confident God had just granted my request for a new best friend. And I was right.

Jimmy Ray had a wonderful sense of humor and was a joy to be around. He was always doing something unexpected and just a bit mischievous. He used to lie in wait just behind his dorm room window. As soon as he spied someone skinny passing by, he would yell, "Hey, you need to eat some mashed potatoes!" then duck so as not to be caught.

Most of his antics were more spontaneous, though. He had a knack for interjecting the right kind of humor at just the right time regardless the topic of conversation. You couldn't spend more than five minutes with him before you found yourself laughing, or at the least snickering with amusement. He loved being with people and loved making them smile, and he nearly always succeeded with his off-the-wall, unexpected humor and his light-hearted, bright outlook on life.

Jimmy Ray and I began spending more and more time together. Money was tight for both of us, so we would spend our time taking walks, going to a nearby zoo, or just watching TV with a bowl of popcorn. In the

Dave, Lynn, Jimmy Ray
December
1985

beginning, I had no romantic interest in him. But that would eventually change.

His roommate Dave often joined Jimmy Ray and me, and the three of us shared a great rapport. The two guys started attending the monthly radio broadcasts I was involved in with Heart Song, and we would go out for ice cream afterward. It was on just such an occasion my first opportunity to meet Jimmy Ray's parents and visit his home presented itself. It was actually a rescue.

Apparently the announcement had gone out that the student life committee was sponsoring a "Get-Your-Roommate-A-Date" event. I'm not sure if it was because she thought me desperate or if she just disliked me, but my roommate set me up with a terribly unlikely candidate without my knowledge. The young man she had asked to go out with me wasn't a bad person, but it would have been obvious to anyone who knew us that we were completely mismatched. I wondered if she had done it just for spite. It seemed to me she thought of herself in a higher social class than I, and it created antagonism between us at times.

The young man called me to set up a time and place for our date. Not wanting to hurt his feelings, I agreed to go out with him weekend after next. I don't think he wanted to go out with me any more than I wanted to go out with him, but we both felt trapped. It was not the intention of either of us to make the other feel rejected.

After the radio broadcast, as we were headed out for ice cream, I shared my dilemma with Jimmy Ray and Dave. They both found my quandary amusing, but Dave took greater pleasure in ribbing me about it. Jimmy Ray, on the other hand, while amused, seemed to want to rescue me.

"I know how you can get out of your date!" Jimmy Ray exclaimed.

"How?" I asked.

"I'm going home to see my parents that weekend. You can come home with me. Just call the guy up and tell him you're going out of town. Problem solved."

"Hmm," I thought, "it would solve my problem." Besides, Jimmy Ray and I had become such wonderful friends; I thought it would be nice to meet his family. I had one hesitation, though. I had the suspicion Jimmy Ray's feelings for me were growing, and I feared mine were growing for him as well. He was a joyful person, full of personality – the kind of person who brings a room to life just by walking into it. Besides that, he treated me like a queen. Who wouldn't be attracted to that kind of person? But he was preparing for pastoral ministry, and that gave me pause.

Another reason I hadn't been attracted to Jimmy Ray earlier was that he lacked a certain discipline I was looking for in a soul mate. He hadn't been serious about his studies, and he lacked a professional persona, even when the occasion called for it. However, something had changed in him over the past few months, and the transformation was evident. Sometime during his junior year Jimmy Ray had come to realize that graduation was fast approaching, and he would soon be seeking a ministry position. He wanted to be taken seriously, and he knew that meant exercising greater discipline and striving for a new level of excellence in every area of his life.

The transformation began with his studies. He began to apply himself academically, and his grades quickly improved. He then moved on to his health. He had been nearly 100 pounds overweight, and feared his appearance might hinder a potential employer's first impression of him. So he got serious about eating healthily and exercising rigorously and regularly. By the time he invited me to his parents' home, he had already dropped nearly 30 pounds. He would drop the other 70 over the next year. His new pursuit of excellence was both apparent and attractive to me.

My list of excuses for not dating him was growing shorter. This created a dilemma for me, and spawned a great emotional conflict. I didn't want to have feelings for Jimmy Ray. He was preparing for pastoral ministry and I wanted to avoid that life at all costs. Yet, here was a man I adored, felt at ease with, and who made me feel cherished. I hadn't forgotten the whisper I had heard the day I met him either – that "heads up" I had gotten from God that this man could be my future husband. The question was, should I explore a more serious relationship with Jimmy Ray and risk a future I had tried so desperately to avoid, or retreat to a safer distance and avoid that path altogether. I would choose to take the risk.

I took Jimmy Ray up on his rescue offer, and agreed to spend the weekend with his family. We loaded up his red Datsun pick-up and headed toward his home. It would prove to be a trip of destiny.

We took the interstate for the first hour or so before having to get off on some smaller, two-lane roads. The closer we got to his home, the more rural the roads became. We were on a stretch of secluded highway when we spotted something in the middle of the road.

"What's that?" I asked. We drove a few seconds more before Jimmy Ray discerned what it was.

"It's a turtle," he said.

"Oh, no!" I said. "It's gonna to get run over."

Jimmy Ray slowed the truck and pulled off to the side of the road as we neared the turtle. Without saying a word, he checked for traffic and hopped out of the truck. He made his way to the middle of the highway, picked up the turtle and set it down safely in a grassy patch on the side of the road.

"Well that was a sweet thing to do," I said.

"Well, I couldn't just leave it there to get run over," he replied.

Jimmy Ray's compassionate nature was just one more thing that attracted me to him.

Before long we arrived at our destination. Jimmy Ray's parents lived in a fieldstone house on a small farm in Northwest Arkansas. It was a peaceful setting, about a half-mile down a dirt road, away from the main highway.

There were a myriad of landmarks that defined it as a farm. Set back from the road on the west side of the property was a deep pond from which the livestock drank. Beyond the pond stood a striking red barn, weathered but freshly painted. A tin roof that extended from a silver metal shop sheltered an assortment of tractors and farm implements. A maze of barbed wire fences served to separate the pasture from the yard and the different animal breeds from one another.

To the east of the house was planted a bountiful garden with everything from tomatoes to potatoes and from corn to squash. Jimmy Ray's mother had been busy painting the yard with the seasons' most vibrant colors, and flowers were starting to bloom in every direction. As you exited the back screen door, which squeaked when opened and banged loudly behind you when it closed, there stood a towering maple tree. Underneath the maple stood a swing set and a picnic table painted red.

The Severns had quite an assortment of animals as well. They had a female cat with no tail named Max. She was one of about a dozen. They had two Australian shepherds – a male named Laddie and a female named Bob. There were plenty of chickens and a rooster that crowed at the crack of dawn. Several horses lined the fencerow as they were offered a special blend of feed that, to them tasted like dessert. Roaming the pasture beyond were at least a couple dozen cows.

I finally had the pleasure of meeting Jimmy Ray's parents. His mother's name was Carol. She was an attractive woman; about five feet six inches tall with a strong but trim build. She had a slim nose, high cheekbones and bronze skin, evidence of time spent working in the sun. It was obvious where Jimmy Ray had gotten his attractive facial features. The resemblance was striking. Her demeanor was as attractive as her outward appearance. She was open, friendly, and welcomed me as one of the family the minute I took my first step through the door.

I met Jimmy Ray's dad a little later in the day. His name was George Thomas, but his family called him Tommy George, or just Tom for short. He looked to be about six feet tall with a handsome face and dark but thinning hair. His face and arms, like Carol's, were dark from tending to his outdoor chores. He had been a Navy man and had a number of tattoos he had collected during his days of active duty. He was a hard-working man, nearing retirement from his main job as a telephone repairman, and he ran a hay cutting business with his uncle during the summer months.

The Severns were hard-working, kind-hearted people--the kind of people you want to sit out on the porch and drink a glass of iced tea with at the end of a long day. I immediately felt at home.

Jimmy Ray and I had a fun-filled weekend. First, we shot coffee cans off the fence with a shotgun. I had never shot a firearm before and found the experience quite exciting. In his usual mischievous fashion, Jimmy Ray instructed me to hold the stock away from my shoulder when I shot. I didn't know any better at the time and proceeded to do as I was instructed. But his softer side got the better of him, and knowing it would kick back and possibly give me a nasty bruise, he stopped me before I pulled the trigger and told me to hug it close to my shoulder to absorb any recoil.

I was also allowed to climb aboard old Bonnie, one of their oldest, most dependable horses. Bonnie could tell right away she was carrying a novice rider, as she kept running me into the fence, regardless of my best attempts to lead her in another direction.

After my short stint on Bonnie, Jimmy Ray took me to one of his favorite spots about a mile down the dirt road from his Granny's house. It was a low-water bridge that went across Flint Creek. Flint was a shallow, spring-fed creek lined with trees on either side that had created a canopy over the water. Jimmy Ray had been baptized here in the middle of winter when he was a young teen. The expression on his face told me this was a special place in his heart and memory.

Carol was a fabulous cook and that first evening she fixed a traditional country dinner: fried chicken, mashed potatoes with gravy, homemade biscuits, a lovely garden salad and home-canned green beans seasoned with bacon. She topped it off with a carrot cake made from scratch. Every bite was a tasty treat.

After dinner, as I helped Carol wash the dishes, I noticed Jimmy Ray was missing. By this time, the sun was just about to set. I asked Carol if she knew where he had gone.

"Oh, he had a little errand to take care of," she responded.

About ten minutes later Jimmy Ray walked through the back door. "Come with me," he said.

He took my hand and led me down through the orchard, past the metal shop and over to the pond. He had built a little bonfire and had hot cocoa and marshmallows for roasting ready to go. He had gathered a few long, thin sticks and whittled a sharp point on the end to use as roasting skewers. I thought it a sweet gesture and the sentiment made me feel special.

The next day I woke up to a sun-shiny, Sunday morning. Today I would get to see the church Jimmy Ray grew up in and also meet his Granny. George was not a churchgoer at the time. He'd grown up with little use for church or preachers. In fact, he had objected strongly when Jimmy Ray announced his plans to go into ministry, thinking it only a phase. But he changed his mind when he saw how strongly Jimmy Ray felt about his call from God and how determined he was to follow that call. George would eventually find his faith in God, but for now he would stay behind while Carol, Jimmy Ray and I went on to Sunday school.

The little country church reminded me of so many other rural churches I had seen. It was a rectangular block building painted white and had steps that led up to a wooden door. When you stepped inside you entered a small vestibule with a men's and women's restroom on opposite sides. As you peered ahead you could see into a long narrow sanctuary with long, dark wooden pews and red shag carpet. On the back wall hung a wooden sign where they posted the last two weeks' attendance and the previous Sunday's offering.

I soon had the privilege of meeting Granny, Jimmy Ray's maternal grandmother. She was quite a lady! There was no mistaking this was a woman full of spunk and vigor. She had a strong handshake and a strong, sure voice. She welcomed me like I was her own, just like George and Carol had. But what I remember most about her was how happy she looked sitting on the platform playing her hot pink, electric guitar and belting out her favorite hymns in her robust alto voice.

After church Jimmy Ray's family, along with Carol's sister's family, met at Granny's house for Sunday dinner. Between Granny, Carol and Carol's twin sister Cathy, they put on a spread that would rival any Thanksgiving feast.

As soon as dinner was over and the dishes had been washed, it was time for a good, old-fashioned family-sing. Carol sat down at the piano and played and sang while Granny and Cathy harmonized. The rest of us joined in here and there where we knew the words. The afternoon felt a bit like being in a Norman Rockwell painting. It was a picture-perfect, family Sunday.

The weekend went by quickly and soon it was time to return to school. Sunday evening we loaded the pickup and headed back. It had been both an eventful and pleasant weekend. As we drove into the night my eyes began to get heavy, so I leaned over and laid my head on the armrest between our seats. Jimmy Ray put his hand on my shoulder and patted it periodically. I found it both a sweet and welcome gesture. There was no turning back from this point. We had developed a special bond we knew would only grow. And it did.

Neither Jimmy Ray nor I could afford to dine out often or attend expensive concerts, so we found more creative, less expensive ways to spend time together. One thing we did often was to visit the largest mall in town. Window-shopping is lots of fun, at least for most women, and easy on the pocket book. On one such trip to the mall Jimmy Ray and I entered through one of the larger department stores. We went in through the women's section, which was of particular interest to me. Jimmy Ray proudly took my hand and we went on our way. I remember getting distracted by some glamorous display of purses or jewelry, Jimmy Ray still holding my hand. As I eyed the display to my left, I felt Jimmy Ray tugging on my right hand. I turned around just in time to see him start to put *my* finger up *his* nose. And though I quickly pulled my hand away when I realized what he was doing, I found his gesture amusing; it made me laugh. It was just one more of his many boyish, playful antics that endeared him to me. I loved his boyish humor.

Jimmy Ray could be mischievous, but he was also thoughtful. He did his internship that following summer of 1986 at a church in Paris, Illinois. It was only two hours from my home in Indiana, and he drove over to visit me once or twice a month. I remember being disappointed the weekend of my birthday, though. He phoned to say he would be later than usual. I wasn't sure why he couldn't be there at his normal time, but I appreciated that he was considerate enough to let me know he wouldn't be there until later in the evening.

43

When he got to my house, he proudly presented me with a gold, thin-banned, sand-dollar ring. My eyes lit up as he slipped it on my finger. I had seen the ring in a little gift shop in Nashville, Indiana, where my mom and I worked during the summers. I had admired the ring and mentioned it to Jimmy Ray just in passing. I had no idea he would buy it, or that he would even remember my mentioning it. He had driven an extra two hours to purchase the ring for me. It was my special day, and he had made the extra long journey to present me with a special gift just because he loved me and knew it would make me smile.

Our dating life was mostly uninterrupted for nearly a year. I knew where we were headed, though, and it scared me at times. I still didn't want to be a pastor's wife, and that aversion prompted me to break up with Jimmy Ray at least twice before we were finally engaged our last semester. I could never stay away from him for very long, though. Our relationship felt right to me, and I knew it had been written in to God's story for our lives.

I remember well the night he proposed. It was February of 1987 and we were visiting his parents in Arkansas. The weekend started off pretty much like any weekend we spent at the Severns. Jimmy Ray and I went inside the house for whatever snack Carol had ready for us and then drove around the countryside until dinnertime. Carol put on her usual country dinner spread, and I helped her with the dishes afterward. Then we all sat around and watched television until George and Carol retired for the evening.

Jimmy Ray and I always stayed up to watch Magnum P.I., which came on the TV somewhere around 11 p.m. We were about 15 minutes into Magnum when a commercial came on. Jimmy Ray got up, turned the TV volume all the way down, came back over to the couch and sat down next to me. He reached in his pocket and retrieved a black velvet box containing a dainty but stunning engagement ring. He had done a remarkable job of choosing one to suit me. It had a round diamond in the middle and four smaller diamonds on either side of the main stone.

He extended his hand and offered me the ring. He had not prepared a long, flowery speech. His proposal was to-the-point but heartfelt.

"I love you, Lynn. Will you marry me?"

I grinned from ear to ear, nodded my head and responded with, "Mmm-hmm." He then slipped the ring onto my finger.

It may not go down in the history books as the most elaborate proposal, or the most romantic acceptance, especially when set against the backdrop of a detective show. But I always look back on the occasion with a smile and with pride for having been loved by someone so special.

It was a happy time, and I was eager to get back to school so I could share the news and show off my engagement ring.

After graduation, we went to our respective homes for the summer before we married in September. It was a difficult summer, as the time apart once again set up doubts in my mind. I loved Jimmy Ray, but I knew saying yes to him also meant saying yes to pastoral ministry. I needed reassurance from God one more time before I took that walk down the aisle and said yes to my groom, yes to God, and yes to a life that had me apprehensive at best. Yet I was confident that if God had ordained our marriage, it was right, and he would give us the wisdom and the courage to face whatever came our way.

God was faithful to whisper reassurance to me. Only this time, it came not as a still small voice in my mind and heart, but through a Bible passage with words specific to my prayer. Hearing God's whisper through his Word was new to me at the time, but it would become customary in the years ahead. I lay on my bed with my Bible in hand and prayed, "Oh, God am I doing the right thing? Is it really your desire that I marry Jimmy Ray? You know I don't want to be a pastor's wife, but if Jimmy Ray and I can bring more people to you together than we can apart, then let it be."

As soon as I had prayed, God directed me to a passage of scripture specific to my prayer. I opened my Bible and my eyes fell upon this verse in Matthew 7:11 (NIV). It simply read, "If you, then, though you are evil, know how to give good gifts to your children, how much more will your Father in heaven give good gifts to those who ask him!" My mind was set at rest. God had answered through his Word. He was telling me that he was giving me a good gift in Jimmy Ray. And he was right.

Jimmy Ray and I were married on September 5th, 1987. The sun shone so bright that day, as though it were beaming down from the smile of God's own face. The day was perfect, and I felt God's peace from the moment I awoke.

My father walked me down the aisle, and my brother Billy presided over the ceremony. I said yes that day. Yes to Jimmy Ray, yes to God, and yes to an adventure I had yet to comprehend.

CHAPTER FIVE

Spiritual Sons and Daughters

Jimmy Ray was fortunate enough to find a youth ministry position in June before we married in September. As God would have it, the church was in Rogers, Arkansas, only 30 minutes from his parents' farm. And although our new position took me nearly 600 miles from my own family, we felt blessed that a door had been open to us so close to his.

It didn't take long for me to feel the weight of others' expectations, though. Only days after Jimmy Ray began work at the church, but before we were married, an older woman from the congregation asked Jimmy Ray, "So...what's your new wife gonna do for *us*?"

I bristled when he relayed her remark to me. I hadn't even moved to the area or met anyone from the church, and they were already more interested in what I was going to *do* or how I was going to perform than who I *was*, or so I thought. It helped to know that Jimmy Ray, who was all too aware of my hesitancy to enter ministry, had already determined not to allow anyone except him and me to dictate what my role would be. That trait would become increasingly important to me as we moved on in ministry. However, the misgivings I already had about my new role, coupled with the woman's comment, caused me to start life as a minister's wife with trepidation and a guarded heart.

My misgivings about life in ministry were compounded by the fact we had to cut our honeymoon short in order to sing at a church-sponsored banquet. It seemed to me a less essential part of the program and one that could easily have been filled by another vocalist. But this was Jimmy Ray's first ministry assignment, and he was eager to please his new pastor. So he agreed to be back before the end of the week in order that we could perform at the banquet. We hadn't been married a week, and already I felt I was competing with the church for my husband's time.

The first several months were difficult at best. The previous youth minister had left involuntarily due to misconduct. He was dearly loved by at least a segment of the youth group, and they were not eager to receive someone new in his place. It mattered not how fervently we reached out to them. There were some who simply would not open their hearts to us. There were, however, others who embraced us. At the time, we could not conceive the impact we would make on their lives. Nor could we know how the love and ministry we poured into them would return to us like a boomerang at our time of greatest need.

Jimmy Ray and I never had children of our own. It wasn't because we were medically incapable. It just seemed we never wanted to start a family at the same time, and neither of us was willing to force such a life-altering decision on the other. I had prayed often that if God wanted us to start a family, he would put the desire in both our hearts at the same time. Yet it never happened and, despite the disapproval and displeasure we endured from others for our decision, I see this now as God's wisdom. There was another reason for my hesitancy to start a family. It stemmed from a foreboding I developed sometime in my early 20's that I would be a young widow. At the time, I had a low-paying, part-time job at the Wal-

Mart home office. It would be a struggle, if not impossible to take care of myself, let alone a child, if I were left without a husband to help support the family. I was determined not to have children until I felt certain I could support them on my own, should anything happen to Jimmy Ray.

But God did not leave us childless. Over the next ten years we would pour our lives into a group of young people who will forever be known as our "kids." They are our spiritual sons and daughters. In much the same way a child cares for a parent when they become too old or sick to care for themselves, our kids would take care of us when we needed them most. We will come back to this later in the story.

Annette was the first to open her arms to us. She was a petite 14 year-old with long, permed hair and windbreaker bangs, typical of the late 1980's. She had a tender heart but a determined spirit and exhibited a work ethic befitting a woman twice her age. We often drove her home from youth events where she received a regular scolding from us for not wearing a coat, even in the dead of winter. Annette was our first girl.

Pastor Brummett had four children. The two oldest were already adults, but their youngest son CJ, also 14 at the time, and his older sister Julie were part of the youth group. CJ was a stereotypical pastor's kid who took pleasure in antagonizing Jimmy Ray to the point of wrath. CJ would do this in a host of ways, until Jimmy Ray would resort to chasing him around the building, voicing threats of a good beating, if only he could catch him. CJ was mischievous, but we loved him and saw in him an unusual tenderness toward God. We knew if he were ever to harness and focus his energy toward ministry, God would use him to touch countless lives with the love of Christ. But I believe CJ, like me, having an insider's view of ministry, was reluctant to follow that path. CJ was our first boy.

Julie was CJ's older sister. She was 19 and attending college at the time, but she remained active in the church and served as a youth sponsor. Since Julie was closer to our age, she became a confidant to me, as well as one of our kids. She had a robust alto voice, and although everything from her blonde hair to her ivory complexion said "white girl," she landed a spot in an African American soul choir on her campus. We loved hearing them perform, and we loved singing with Julie ourselves. She gave our trio soul.

Frankie was Annette's younger sister. She was only 10 when we arrived, but we were youth ministers at Rogers First Assembly (RFA) for eight years and had the privilege of watching her grow to adulthood. On one particular evening toward the end of the youth service, I felt as though God were telling me he had a special ministry prepared for Frankie. I shared this insight with Jimmy Ray later that evening; he concurred. She had a passion for children's ministry I have seen in few people. She was the kind of girl who wanted to embrace every child she could find who was hurting and tell them how Jesus could make it better. We had no inkling at the time how the special ministry God had prepared for her would one day intertwine with ours.

Jimmy Ray developed a heart and passion for mentoring young people, and his style of mentorship was one that drew others to him. His approach was casual rather than clinical. He preferred to impart wisdom over a cup of coffee or a Coke rather than from behind a desk, although he engaged in both. He had a goofy sense of humor and a smile as bright as sunshine that set people at ease. Even though he was perhaps best known for his jocularity, he had a sincere concern for his kids and a God-given wisdom well beyond his years.

Brad, Rick, Ken and Mylon were a group of young men who made the most of every opportunity to be mentored by Jimmy Ray. They were at the age when important and sometimes difficult life decisions were being made, and they knew whatever quandary or dilemma they were facing, they could count on Jimmy Ray for a wise word, a fervent prayer, and an arm around the shoulder. Brad would eventually find himself pursuing missions work abroad. Ken would champion a children's home for foster children in Northwest Arkansas, and all four of these young men would become model husbands and fathers.

Jimmy Ray was an accomplished bass player, and was "eat up," as he would put it, with all things guitar. His love of music, and guitars in particular, inspired another young man, Darrell, to take up the trade. Darrell even looked a little like Jimmy Ray. They were both slim, had thick blonde hair, and wore their hair in what Jimmy Ray referred to as a Ph.D., or Pentecostal hairdo, typical of big-haired preachers in the late 1980's. Darrell became his protégé and a very proficient bass player in his own right. I still have pictures of the two of them playing guitars together out at the Severn barn, where we had worship services after a bonfire and hayride on the farm.

There was Mary, whose last name started with "G", but we called her Mary Ray Cyrus because she was smitten with the singer, Billy Ray Cyrus, and wore her hair in a mullet to resemble his. Last I heard, Mary, who no longer wears her hair in a mullet, was pursuing a career in nursing.

Matt was a tender hearted young man who was well over six feet tall and tipped the scales at around 300 by the time he was 15 years old. Jimmy Ray, who was five feet six inches tall and weighed around 130 by this time, having dropped 100 pounds in college, was blessed with the honor of baptizing Matt. Jimmy Ray was overjoyed to take part in this step of Matt's spiritual journey.

Jimmy Ray knew the size difference might prove a challenge when it came time to baptize Matt. So he put a footstool in the baptistery to stand on to get a better hold on Matt's shoulders as he lowered him into the water. Let's just say, Matt got away from him.

There was a group of feisty junior high girls we referred to as "the little girls" because they were considerably younger than the rest of the group. I used to pick them up in my car for youth service, because they had gotten into mischief and been banned from riding the church van. One of these girls, Coreen, had survived leukemia as a small child. She was a pretty girl, but she was tall for her age, painfully thin, and had very long, thick black hair. Jimmy Ray, who took special pleasure in dolling out nicknames, called her "Morticia" because she reminded him of Morticia from "The Adams Family." She would later pursue a career in nursing, as she had been touched by the care she had received as a child in the hospital.

Then there were Jennifer and Steve. They were rebellious in the beginning, and as does happen from time to time, had a baby together before they married. But on their wedding day, they took Jimmy Ray aside, told him how God had transformed their hearts, and how from that they day forward they were going to serve God together as a family. And they did just that. In fact, they would later follow us as youth ministers at RFA when we resigned to take a position in another state. Jennifer and Steve would go on to raise three beautiful children and enjoy many years of effective full-time ministry.

Much to my surprise, I found myself enjoying ministry at RFA. I cherished the bond I had formed with these kids and found joy in being part of their lives. The church had accepted me for who I was and allowed me to minister through my strengths rather than criticizing me in areas where I lacked. I even found the older woman, who had questioned Jimmy Ray about what my role in the church would be, to be very kind and completely accepting of me. I had entered ministry braced for attack, but I had been embraced instead.

Jimmy Ray was asked to lead worship for the adults on Sundays, and I accompanied him on the piano. For youth services, Jimmy Ray played both the acoustic and electric guitars, as we strived to provide a more contemporary worship experience for the kids. Leading people into the presence of God through music and worship became a passion for Jimmy Ray. Although he felt somewhat stifled in his worship ministry at RFA due to the older demographic of the congregation, a time would later come when Jimmy Ray had the freedom to lead others in worship with the exuberance and passion for God that burned inside his heart.

I looked on with pride as I watched Jimmy Ray grow during our time at RFA. The new discipline he had developed in college was paying off, and his pursuit of excellence in every area of his life was evident. He grew in his ability to teach, to preach, to lead worship, to mentor young people, and to do it all in new and creative ways. He began to hone new skills in sound engineering, recording, and even graphic design. In all this, God was preparing him for a greater task ahead.

In 1993, six years into our ministry at RFA, we began to feel a change in ministry was on the horizon. We began to pray for God's direction and opened our hearts to whatever ministry God had waiting for us.

During that same year my father was diagnosed with colon cancer.

Pastor Brummett and his wife Doris delivered the heart-wrenching news to me. Dad had always been a rock for me, and the one I went to whenever I needed guidance or advice. I could scarcely fathom life without him should the disease claim his life.

Dad needed surgery to remove a very large tumor in his colon, so Jimmy Ray and I made the trip back to Indiana for the surgery. I chose to stay with my family the Sunday following the surgery, but Jimmy Ray decided to attend church. Rather than go to my home church in Bloomington, he attended Ellettsville First Assembly in the next town over where he was reasonably sure he would not to be recognized. Up-front ministry can be draining at times, and once in awhile, it's nice to simply be another face in the crowd.

A woman in the church spotted him as a visitor and introduced herself. When she discovered he was a youth minister visiting from out of town, she introduced him to the pastor. Pastor Cain took him aside and said, "I don't think you're here by accident." He proceeded to explain to Jimmy Ray that their youth pastor had just resigned. Pastor Cain felt perhaps God had ordained Jimmy Ray's being there that day because he was to be their next youth minister.

We made arrangements to meet with Pastor Cain a week or two later. We felt drawn to the church, but we didn't feel the timing was right and declined to pursue the position further. The church itself, however, remained in our hearts.

Over the next two years, we would interview with six more pastors in six different states as we sought God's direction. However it seemed the churches we were drawn to were not drawn to us. Conversely, we did not feel God's leading to go to the churches that invited us to come. Those two years of limbo were a frustrating time for us, as I'm sure they were for Pastor Brummett. But we were willing to wait until God opened the door of his choosing and said, "Enter."

One day, as I was asking God for his direction, I opened up to this verse in Revelation 3:7-8 (NIV). "…What he [God] opens, no one can shut, and what he shuts no one can open…See, I have placed before you an open door that no one can shut." God whispered to me that day that he would open a door for us, and he would make it clear to all that it was the door of his choosing.

The call came in the spring of 1995. I can't precisely remember where we had been, but when we returned home, there was a message waiting for us on the answering machine. It was Pastor Cain from the Ellettsville church where Jimmy Ray had visited two years prior. Apparently, the youth minister they had hired was leaving, and the position was open once again. The minute I heard Pastor Cain's voice, God whispered, "This is it." Ellettsville was the right place, and this was the right time. After a weekend interview we accepted the position.

Ellettsville First Assembly was only 10 miles from my home. While I had thoroughly enjoyed being close to Jimmy Ray's parents, I was thankful to be going back home to mine. My father had been battling cancer for two years now. Not only had he had part of his colon and bladder removed, the cancer had spread to his liver and half of it had been removed as well. I didn't know how long I would have my dad, and I wanted to be close to home while he battled this disease.

After eight years of ministry at RFA, we said good-bye to our "kids." We had been with them through those tough junior high years, through crushes and break-ups, through marriages, divorces, and the birth of new children. Our hearts had swelled with pride as we watched many of them grow in their relationship with Christ. Our hearts were broken when others made decisions that took them far from Christ and eventually caused them pain. For good or for ill these were our kids, and we loved them, no matter what. But Jimmy Ray and I had been called to another group of kids, and we were ready to go.

Jimmy Ray often felt he had failed at RFA because our youth group never grew to more than 25 or 30 in average attendance. But as we would later find, he was far from a failure. He had birthed a generation of spiritual sons and daughters, and the fruit of his labor would become evident in the years to come.

CHAPTER SIX

LIVING IN A FISH BOWL

We loaded up a moving van, and with the help of Jimmy Ray's parents we moved to Ellettsville, Indiana, in March of 1995. Although it was difficult to leave behind beloved family members, friends, and those we called our "kids," I was happy to be moving home. I wanted to be near my family while my father battled cancer.

The transition was more difficult for Jimmy Ray. I remember the first moments after his parents pulled out of the drive and headed back to Arkansas. I found Jimmy Ray sitting on the floor of an empty back bedroom. His eyes were red, and he was wiping tears from his smooth, ruddy cheeks. The Severns were a close-knit family, and Jimmy Ray knew time between visits would now be measured in months rather than days or weeks. It broke his heart to be so far from home. But God had opened this door for us, and we were ready to make the sacrifices necessary in order to meet the challenges of our new ministry.

Our youth ministry started at Ellettsville much the same way it had at RFA in Rogers. The former youth minister had left involuntarily and the kids were not eager to accept someone new in his place. As hard as it was to break through the emotional barriers we encountered at RFA, it was even harder here. One young man summed up the feeling of a large part of the group when he snidely told Jimmy Ray to his face, "We don't want you here. Why don't you just go back to Arkansas?"

The youth group attendance was somewhere around 50 or 60 when we started at the church. I think we successfully shrank the group to about half in the first six months; but Pastor Cain was supportive. He knew Jimmy Ray was leading the youth into God's presence through worship and teaching them sound Biblical truth each week. And he, like us, was certain God had arranged our being there and was willing to ride out the storm with us until the ministry stabilized.

Sometime that summer, I landed a job processing student payroll for the Indiana University (IU) Library system. This was a special blessing to me, as my father was also working on campus. His office was just down the road from mine, so we often met for lunch. It took me back to times I had spent with my dad from grade school through high school. Every so often, he would come to my door as I was getting ready to catch the bus and say, "If you get ready a little early this morning, I'll take you to McDonald's for breakfast." Those were some of my most cherished memories, and God had granted me the opportunity to enjoy these special father/daughter times once again.

Jimmy Ray and I had grown close over the first eight years of our marriage and ministry. Aside from the normal adjustments couples experience as they attempt to meld two lives into one, we rarely had a disagreement. My work schedule in Rogers had been flexible enough for me to take off the same day as Jimmy Ray, so we had at least one day through the week and most Saturdays together. We had grown to adore each other and loved spending our days off together. As a couple, we were living happily ever after.

But our new assignment at Ellettsville came with new challenges. More was required of both of us, and the stress would eventually take its toll. Due to a rigid payroll schedule, I was not always able to take off work the same day Jimmy Ray did. Jimmy Ray was required to work half days on Saturday and often had to mow the church lawn after office hours. Sundays, of course, were full for both of us. His new responsibilities and work schedule cut in on time we had always spent together.

About six months after we arrived, the pastor scheduled a 10-day revival. It evolved into an eight-week revival. I was working all day and spending all evening, sometimes until 10 p.m. or later at the church. Jimmy Ray assisted with worship, along with Pastor Cain, and I was playing the piano for both worship and altar services most nights. I felt I had no choice but to be at every service, at least for the first few weeks. It was exhausting.

It is not my intention to paint an entirely negative picture of this time, however. As at Rogers, we did have a small number of youth at Ellettsville who appreciated and responded to our ministry. They too, would become our kids. As for the outcomes of the revival, many of our teens, as well as Jimmy Ray and I, were changed for life during those two months. I would not dare take that experience away from any of us who were transformed by God during that time.

Jimmy Ray also enjoyed a new freedom to lead worship with the exuberance and passion for God that had been shut up inside him for so long – something that had been discouraged at RFA due to an older demographic. I'm not sure I've ever seen anyone lead worship with more passion than Jimmy Ray. He would strap his guitar around his neck, and play and sing with all his might. Then, as he would get caught up in his expression of love to God, he would lift both arms out to God. Like David in the Bible, his joy would often overflow into a dance before his Lord and he would jump up and down in place, looking upward toward heaven as though he were peering into God's own face. He had a connection to God I've seen few others enjoy because he had the courage to forget everything around him and just go after God with his whole being. Leading others into God's presence through passionate worship would prove to be a hallmark of his ministry.

Jimmy Ray leading worship

Those first two years were a time of both blessings and challenges. I enjoyed being close to family and enjoyed the role I had been given in the church's music ministry. But I struggled with a lack of confidence in other areas. I had difficulty relating to this group of teens and felt my ministry to them was ineffective. I felt like a reluctant traveler lost in a foreign land in this role, and couldn't understand why God had ever led me down the path of full-time ministry. Yes, I could play the piano and sing. But being a minister's wife is so much more than that, and I felt I was failing the church and the youth in the areas that were most vital.

I went to the pastor one afternoon before that night's revival service. I talked with him about my reluctance to enter ministry and the struggle I was having being in that role. I felt I was failing in the area of ministry that counted most – one on one, personal ministry. My timid nature made connecting with the ones Jimmy Ray and I were responsible for a constant, arduous struggle. I felt the constant weight of others' expectations and longed to hide away in a place that was safe from the public eye. The pastor gave me encouraging counsel and prayed with me. But I went to that evening's service feeling the same weight and wrestling with the same question. "Why, God, did you put me here?"

At the close of that evening's service, I went forward for prayer. After the evangelist had prayed for me, I sat down on the front pew on the right side of the sanctuary. I could take you to the very spot.

A woman I had never met was sitting directly behind me. I felt her hands as she laid them gently on my shoulders. She sat there praying silently for just a moment. Then she leaned forward and began to speak quietly into my ear. I don't remember every word or detail, but she began to address every issue I had raised in the pastor's office that day. I knew there was no way she could have known the content of that conversation. God was the only one who could have revealed to her what I needed to hear that night, and it was he who was whispering encouragement to me through this dear lady.

Although I have forgotten much of what she shared, there was one message she relayed that never left me, and one I would not understand the meaning of until many years later. She said, "God has something for you to do that nobody else can do." Warm tears flowed down my face as I began to weep. I was overwhelmed by the concern of such a magnificent God. He knew me, he loved me, and he wanted to help me. The awareness of both his concern for and his confidence in me brought comfort to my troubled heart.

However, as comforted as I felt, I couldn't think of one thing I could do for God that someone else couldn't do better. There were plenty of people who were more outgoing, better spoken, and better musicians than I. "How am I unique?" I wondered. The only role I could think of that was unique to me was that of Jimmy Ray's wife. I wasn't the only minister's wife, but I was the only minister's wife married to Jimmy Ray. I couldn't comprehend how God could possibly use that unique position for something significant. Yet I tucked that little message from God away in my heart, and waited for my purpose to unfold.

God changed something in me through the course of that revival. He was building my confidence in the person he had created me to be. He gave me a new peace in my role, although it remained a challenge for me. He had begun that work through a whisper – the whisper of his voice coming through the conduit of a loving servant.

For the next year and a half, we continued to pour God's Word, his wisdom and our love into the lives of those in the youth group. Although our attendance never fully recovered, we saw an increasing spiritual growth and maturity in those kids who came. We could see the evidence of God's work in their lives, and we were thankful.

But the older we got, the less effective we felt in teen ministry. This was true of me more than of Jimmy Ray, but we both began to feel our days of youth ministry were coming to a close. I remember driving home from work one day, and just saying out loud to God, "Oh God, I can't do this [youth ministry] anymore!" Not only was it increasingly difficult for me to relate to this age group, but the constant activity was exhausting. The evening and weekend activities were also eating up any time Jimmy Ray and I might have spent together. It was becoming increasingly difficult to stay connected as a couple; that concerned me.

When I got home from work that evening, I noticed a look of concern on Jimmy Ray's face. "I've got something to tell you," he said with a serious tone. "Pastor Cain is resigning." When he spoke those words, all I heard was, "Your days of full-time youth ministry are over." I breathed a sigh of relief. Jimmy Ray, on the other hand, heard, "You're out of a job." You see, in our church fellowship, it's customary for the staff to resign when the pastor does, and Jimmy Ray was feeling the pressure of finding a new position.

I felt a huge weight lift off me that day. I loved the kids, but I felt they could be better served by a younger couple, and for my part, someone more in tune with their culture. The additional financial compensation often offered to someone in a senior pastoral position also made me hopeful that I would be able to quit work. Having more time to fulfill my church responsibilities as well as spend time with Jimmy Ray appealed to me. I was hopeful for the future.

After Pastor Cain's last service, the church board asked the congregation to spend the next 30 days praying for God's direction in choosing a new minister. They would not make any decisions before the 30 days were up.

Before he left, Pastor Cain suggested to the board that they consider Jimmy Ray to take his place. We were somewhat surprised by the confidence this showed in us, but were excited about the prospect of staying on. We had grown to love this church, and I was excited about the prospect of remaining close to family, particularly in light of Dad's ongoing battle with cancer. We were unsure, however, if the board would even consider Jimmy Ray. He was only 31 at the time and had no prior pastoral experience. The church had between 225 and 250 attendees and the potential for growth. The question was, had Jimmy Ray been responsible and effective enough over the past two years to earn that kind of trust from a church that size. The answer was yes.

In March of 1997, Jimmy Ray was voted in as the new senior pastor of Ellettsville First Assembly. He and I were amazed by all God had done to place us there. It is doubtful Jimmy Ray would ever have been considered for the position had we not been on the ministry staff for two years already. It had given Jimmy Ray the opportunity to prove himself as a loyal, hard-working minister and worship leader with the highest integrity. He was young, but he had both the vision and character this church desired in their next shepherd.

Jimmy Ray hit the ground running. He had two vacancies to fill – administrative assistant and youth minister. Hiring takes time, however, so he tried to fulfill the responsibilities of pastor, youth pastor and administrative assistant himself for the first several months.

61

He led worship and preached on Sundays, continued to oversee the youth ministry, including planning regular youth activities, saw to all the correspondence, prepared the church bulletins, mowed the church lawn, and met all his other pastoral responsibilities. He made regular hospital visits, performed marriages and funerals and occasionally provided pastoral counseling.

Because of personal finances, it was necessary for me to continue working, but by this time my workweek had gone from fulltime to halftime. I was only required to work overtime during the fall or spring when new-hire paperwork was at its peak. The reduction in hours was a blessing for this busy pastor's wife. But while I now had more time off, Jimmy Ray had gone from working 40 hours per week to around 60 or 70 hours per week. Instead of senior pastoral ministry allowing us more time together, as I had hoped, just the opposite resulted. We saw each other less now than before. We began to slowly drift apart.

After interviewing a few temporary office helpers, Jimmy Ray finally hired Carole Brown as his administrative assistant. Carole was a Godsend. Jimmy Ray was the kind of person who wanted assignments carried out with perfection, making it difficult for him to turn any task over to another. But Carole made it her mission to relieve Jimmy Ray of as much responsibility as possible. She would find it a daunting task, but she would eventually succeed, and succeed with the excellence Jimmy Ray demanded.

As Jimmy Ray and I looked at and prayed over resumes from youth ministry candidates, one couple stood out to me – Roger and Sharon Coleman. I don't remember now just what it was about their resume that caught my attention, but I do remember being very drawn to this couple. I pulled their resume out of the stack, showed it to Jimmy Ray and said, "This is the couple. They're the ones," quite sure of my selection. Although, I do believe it would be more accurate to say, "*God's* selection" rather than "*my* selection." Jimmy Ray was curious about my certainty regarding this couple, but after prayerful consideration, he too became convinced they were

God's choice for the position.

I remember the first time we met with Roger. He and Sharon were not yet married and he had to come to the interview alone. We were to meet at Chili's Restaurant in Bloomington. Jimmy Ray and I arrived first. We sat down at a table and began looking over the menus as we waited for Roger to arrive. As we watched out the window, we saw Roger pull up and exit his car. We recognized him from the photo he had sent with his resume. He had an uncertain, nervous look that made his boyish face look even younger. This was obviously his first interview.

We made our introductions and sat down for lunch and a chat. I have no recollection of the details of the conversation, but I remember going away with the impression Roger would be a loyal and hardworking employee. Regardless of their lack of experience, we knew in our hearts Roger and Sharon Coleman were God's choice to be Ellettsville First Assembly's new youth ministers. Jimmy Ray offered them the position, and they accepted. They came to us in May of 1997, just one week after they wed.

I was relieved when Jimmy Ray finally filled the two vacant positions. I hoped it would relieve some of the responsibility he had taken on, but that would not be the case. After he had his staff in place, he simply redirected his attention to other matters. This was Jimmy Ray's first senior ministry assignment, and he was not about to fail. He felt a great responsibility had been entrusted to him, and to meet the challenge with mediocrity was the same as failure to him. However, his pursuit for excellence and his determination to please became an obsession and a detriment, rather than a healthy motivator. He adopted a new, and what I consider a self-destructive slogan. "Good enough never is."

The church building was getting some age on it and was in great need of remodeling and repair. Over the next few years, Jimmy Ray would oversee numerous remodeling projects. When his skills fit the job, he provided much of the labor himself. It was a never-ending and at times all-consuming task. I wondered to myself at times if his unbridled determination and unbalanced work ethic would claim his life as it had my grandfather's.

Jimmy Ray's new work schedule began to take its toll on our relationship. On one particular day, I called the office assistant and asked her to set up an appointment for me to see Jimmy Ray. I told her to use another name because I wanted to be sure he would see me. I was afraid if he knew the appointment was for me, he would tell me to just wait until he got home that evening to see me. Thankfully, I was wrong. When he found out I had resorted to using a false identity to get his attention, he felt terribly guilty. As soon as I arrived at the church, he left the office and took me for a drive over to Nashville, Indiana, the same little town where he had purchased my gold sand-dollar ring when we were dating.

It was a beautiful day. The sun was bright, the leaves were turning and the temperature was neither too hot nor too cold. Despite the beauty of the day, Jimmy Ray wasn't enjoying it at all; he seemed overwhelmed with stress. As we talked about his work, I strongly encouraged him to let go of some of his responsibilities or to dole them out to others. But rather than hearing my concern for him, he took it as a scolding. He pulled off the road, put his head on the steering wheel and with an emphatic, desperate tone instructed, "Stop! You don't understand. This job is too much for me!" But I did understand. I understood the *way* he was doing his job would be too heavy a burden for anybody. He needed to cut himself some slack, stop trying to appease everyone, and delegate more of the responsibility. Yet at the time, he was too young, too inexperienced, and too eager to please to know how to do that successfully. Time and experience would be his teachers.

It was into this time of mounting stress that God sent a little ray of sunshine to both Jimmy Ray and me. It was during the 1999 Ellettsville Fall Festival. Jimmy Ray had spent several hours that evening working in the youth group's tenderloin booth. I had stayed at home.

Sometime around 11:00 p.m. I heard Jimmy Ray pull up in the drive. But unlike any other time he came home, he rang the front door bell rather than come in through the garage. I thought it was peculiar, but I quickly went to the door to let him in. Why he hadn't used his key to let himself in, I didn't know.

"Lynn, I brought you something," he said with a boyish grin. He had his hands behind his back. I assumed he must have stopped by one of the booths at the Festival and bought me a souvenir or a sweet treat.

"You brought me something? What is it?" I inquired.

Without saying a word, he brought his hands out from behind his back. There in his hands was a tiny kitten, no longer than five or six inches long. She was obviously malnourished and infested with fleas, but that seemed to have no affect on her playfulness. She immediately began crawling up Jimmy Ray's coat sleeve and around his neck, purring the entire time.

"What? You brought home a cat?" I had never considered myself a "cat person" and was not eager to become one. But I had a soft spot for furry little creatures and my instinct to take care of this feisty little feline got the better of me. She had a snow-white tummy, a black and brown striped face and sparkling emerald eyes. Her back was mostly brown with a black stripe down the middle. From the long stripe down her back flowed what looked like tiger stripes and a few black spots that wrapped around her sides that were swollen with hunger.

"Well, I guess we can keep her in the garage, but only until we can find a home for her," I said.

Jimmy Ray then told me the story of how he found her. "I was walking from the Festival to the church parking lot where my truck was," he said. "The lot was full and there were a bunch of cars coming and going. Just as I was getting into my truck, I noticed a young couple walking past the church. I couldn't hear what the girl said to the guy, but I saw him turn around and then look at his girlfriend. He said, 'I don't care if it gets run over. It's not my cat!'" Jimmy Ray looked down just then to see the tiniest little kitten following the young couple down the sidewalk. He continued with his story.

"So I said to myself, 'Well, *I* care if she gets run over!'" Jimmy Ray looked at me as though trying to discern whether I shared his concern. "I couldn't just leave her there to get run over."

I was moved by his story and gasped at the young man's callous attitude toward this helpless little kitty. "Let me hold her," I told Jimmy Ray. He took her from behind his neck and handed her to me.

"Let's see if I can find something to make her a bed. Then I'll go to the store and get her some food and a litter box," I said. I then carried her to the garage and found a small carpet remnant left over from when the house was built. I thought it would make a lovely, soft little bed for her. So I laid it out at the front side of the garage near the door to the house and laid her on it. She looked pleased and walked around the carpet with her head and tail sticking straight in the air. Then she showed her appreciation by using it as her toilet. Jimmy Ray and I both laughed at my feeble attempt to make her a bed she approved of. What I thought was a plush, royal bed was no better than a toilet to this persnickety little kitty.

Jimmy Ray and Kitty

I quickly made a trip to the store to pick up a litter box and some kitty food. We would have to make other arrangements for a bed later on.

It took about a week to find someone willing to take this cat we were now calling "Kitty" off our hands. In that short time, she had managed to nudge her way from our garage into the house. We had meant to bring her in only for a few minutes at a time to play with her. But when we tried to put her out, she would always manage to escape. She would run wildly around the house – Jimmy Ray and I both trying frantically to catch her. She would inevitably run behind the refrigerator where neither of us could get to her. We just had to wait until she was ready to come out.

I knew Kitty hated the garage. The tell tale sign was a series of claw marks higher than our heads that donned both sides of the door that separated the garage from the house. Kitty was tiny, but she was full of spirit – spirit we found amusing. We loved the life and humor she brought into the house. So after we had her treated for fleas, we decided to let her stay in the house.

Kitty's entertaining antics as well as her fascination with me (as Jimmy would say, "Kitty's in love with Lynn") made giving her up hard to do. She followed me everywhere I went in the house. She met me when I came home from work. She was at my feet when I worked in the kitchen. She lay across my neck purring at night. When I got ready for work in the mornings, she would curl up in Jimmy Ray's sink while I used mine to wash and put on make-up. If I hadn't known better, I would have sworn it was her plan to soften me up all along. And her plan worked. Not only did she manage to work her way from the garage into the house, this tenacious little kitty had both entertained and purred her way into our hearts. We turned down the offer to take her off our hands and kept her for ourselves. She would be Kitty Severn for many years to come.

All cats must have their prey, and Kitty was no different. But since we kept her indoors, Jimmy Ray and I were the only prey she had to stalk. After a few months of dodging kitty claws, which could come at you from anywhere at any time of the day or night, we decided it was time to get Kitty a playmate.

We got Kitty's new playmate, Noah, from a friend who had just had a baby and found herself too busy to be bothered with a kitten. Noah and I bonded immediately. He was docile and sweet and never offered to bite or scratch. This was quite opposite Kitty who, although at times quite loving, was high-spirited and unpredictable.

Unlike Kitty, whose head seemed too small for her body, Noah's head looked especially large for his tiny frame. In fact, his head was so big he looked as though he could topple head first at any moment. I could just imagine him lying head first on the ground, his little legs dangling in the air – not quite heavy enough to offset the weight of his giant head.

Kitty and Noah provided one small distraction from the busyness and stress of ministry. But Jimmy Ray continued to push himself. Of course everything he did, he did with excellence. From preaching to leading worship, from mentoring his staff to overseeing remodeling projects, and from overseeing church finances to cleaning toilets between janitors, he did everything with excellence. While the stress of his new work schedule began to erode his physical and my emotional health, the church benefited from his hard work. We saw slow but steady growth over the next few years. Our parking lot and sanctuary began to fill up, and talk of a new worship center ensued. Both Jimmy Ray and the board agreed it was time to prepare for expansion. Building a new worship center became Jimmy Ray's newest mission and greatest passion.

By the end of the second year of senior pastoral ministry, our marriage was suffering severely. I was feeling neglected. We needed to spend more time together as a couple, but we couldn't seem to make it happen. Jimmy Ray would at times make plans with me and cancel them at the last minute because someone in the church had planned an activity, and he felt it more important to be attentive to his flock. Other times we would make plans to go out of town, and he would cancel those plans at the last minute because he felt his presence was needed at the church. It left me feeling frustrated and betrayed. The church had become the "other woman" and I felt helpless to compete. But when I tried to talk with him about it, he reacted as though I were only adding to his stress.

My frustration was compounded by the fact I was required to constantly give of myself to support him in his ministry, yet he was unwilling to give of himself to support my emotional needs. It didn't seem fair that I should be making all the sacrifices. And although I never stopped loving him, I became increasingly resentful of both him and the church I felt had stolen him from me.

Matters worsened when Jimmy Ray's stress got the better of him and he began suffering severe headaches. He had them every day for four months. One Sunday, he was in such pain while preaching, he had to hold on to the pulpit with both hands, for fear he might pass out. I took him to the emergency room immediately after the service. He was diagnosed with cluster headaches. They differ from migraines in some respects, but the pain is just as intense. It was all he could do to get dressed and go to work each day, and when he got home, he simply laid on the couch until bedtime.

It hurt me to see him in such pain, but this new health issue put yet another stress on our marriage. I never realized until I lived through it, just how stressful sickness can be for the spouse of the patient. I was receiving little emotional support from Jimmy Ray before he became ill, and now he could give me nothing at all. The fact that I felt his illness could have been avoided by a more balanced approach to work and ministry only fed my resentment. Before I lived through it, I would have considered that attitude in someone else a petty, selfish one. But there are many trials in life that change our perspective and render us less judgmental. I was about to endure another such trial.

I was lonely, often enjoying only the company of Kitty and Noah. The stress of church demands, the ever-expanding emotional gap between Jimmy Ray and me, and now the added demand of caring for an ill spouse were overwhelming. The stresses of ministry, marital, and Jimmy Ray's health issues were compounded by the fact that Dad's battle with cancer was heating up. His colon cancer had spread to his left lung and one-third of it had to be removed. Subsequent x-rays would show new tumors in the right lung as well. I felt weak and ill equipped to manage the emotional weight. It is in those times when we feel weakest and most vulnerable though, that we must be most on our guard against the devil's schemes.

I found myself attracted to an acquaintance I had met at IU. He was never made aware of my feelings, and so to protect his privacy, we will simply call him Ricky. He was attractive, friendly, and single at the time. My job did not require interaction with him on a professional level, but I had regular, job-related contact with others in his department. Ricky always greeted me as I was on my way to see my contacts in his area. Cordial greetings led to friendly chats, which eventually led to a benign friendship. But as emotionally needy as I had become, it was not a far leap from friendship to infatuation. Infatuation would soon escalate into a raging battle to keep my heart and emotions in check.

I despised myself for having feelings for another man. I felt guilty when I was away from Ricky and terribly self-conscious when I was around him. At the same time, his kind attention and innocent compliments fed my hunger for attention. He had a delightful sense of humor, too, and as serious and stressful as my personal life had become, the laughter I enjoyed with him brought a welcome lift to my spirit.

I found myself anticipating my trips to Ricky's department more and more. My feelings for him were growing. But I knew I could not allow these feelings to get out of control. I had to resist them. I had made a vow before God to love, honor, and cherish my husband and to forsake all others when we married. Regardless of the emotional struggle I was having because of Ricky, I knew I had to keep a handle on my feelings. I prayed every day that God would remove the feelings I was developing for Ricky and to please help me keep my words, actions, and emotions in check. Unfortunately, the battle was long and fierce, and I often questioned how strong I would be if Ricky ever expressed a romantic interest in me. Thankfully, God spared me that dilemma.

Up to this point in my life, I couldn't imagine how anyone could be unfaithful to his or her spouse. How could anyone, so in love when they married, become so emotionally detached from their spouse that they actually left them for another? I had thought myself above such temptation. I thought myself too in love with Jesus and too in love with Jimmy Ray to ever wrestle with those kinds of emotions. But God was allowing me a first-hand glimpse of just how easy it is to become so emotionally starved, you find yourself drawn to any source that feeds that hunger. And while God does not tempt his children, I believe he allowed me to suffer temptation in order that I might see those who cross the line from attraction to adultery through more compassionate, less judgmental eyes.

I battled with the contradiction that was my life. There I sat on the platform Sunday after Sunday and Wednesday after Wednesday playing the piano, supporting my husband's ministry. For the sake of the church, I had endured my pain alone from inside the fishbowl. Those looking from without saw what they perceived to be a picture-perfect pastor's wife – faithful, dedicated, submissive. They had no idea there was a raging sea inside, its relentless waves crashing against a slowly breaking heart. And neither they, nor I, could imagine the ferocity of the storm that yet lay ahead.

© 2010 Lynn Severn Blankenship

Barbed Wire Noose

In a little farming town in Arkansas there stands a barn atop a hill. The road that takes you up that hill leads you past a mighty oak. Its trunk is strong and its branches broad. It has weathered many storms. About three feet up from the roots of that tree are remnants of a barbed-wire noose. Its sharp, twisted barbs dig deep into the tree, and the bark is torn and marred.

Can you imagine if the tree had been given voice, from agony how loud it would cry? The passing of time and the growth of the tree forced the barbs to cut deeper inside. The tree has no way of escaping its fate; it quietly must bear this assault.

But the tree has begun to envelop the noose and each year allows less to be seen. It has withstood the assault, and now the noose is surrounded by the trunk of the tree. And while the tree is ever aware of the noose, it no longer feels the pain of those sharp twisted barbs; they've been swallowed up by its life. That thing that once threatened the life of the tree has now become only a part.

Now all that remain are the tail of that wire and the scars left behind on the trunk. They are a testament to the strength of the life in that tree and the enemy over which it triumphed.

CHAPTER SEVEN

LEARNING TO LIVE WITH BARBED WIRE

When I was a young teenager, I came across a verse in Psalms that both amazed and intrigued me. It says, "The LORD confides in those who fear him; he makes his covenant known to them." Psalm 25:14 (NIV). What an amazing thought, that the God of Heaven would "confide" or would share secrets with mortal man.

Being able to discern God's whisper was always important to me. Even as a young girl I prayed God would make me sensitive to his voice and that He would help me always to obey it.

But hearing God's whisper can come with a price. When God speaks, it means God is at work. And when God is at work, our enemy, the devil is often at work to thwart God's purpose. And if you happen to be the conduit through which God chooses to work, you are often the object of the enemy's attack.

The writer of Hebrews tells his audience in chapter 10 (ASV), "But call to remembrance the former days, in which, after ye were enlightened, ye endured a great conflict of sufferings..." The truth is that conflict and suffering often follow God's whisper of revelation. When God reveals something of importance to you, that revelation is often followed by a great battle – one for your very life and soul. I was about to hear a whisper from God that would catapult me into an emotional and spiritual war zone.

It was March of 2001. We had been pastoring Ellettsville First Assembly for four years and I had been quietly struggling with my attraction to Ricky for nearly two years. Jimmy Ray had scheduled a revival at the church and we were sitting in our living room chatting until time to leave for service. Out of the blue, Jimmy Ray said rather matter-of-factly, "I don't think I'm going to live to be an old man."

I was taken aback by the comment. Over the past four years, he had learned to deal more effectively with the stress of his position and was feeling well physically. He hadn't suffered with severe headaches in over two years. Since he wasn't suffering with any apparent medical issues, I thought it strange he would make such a statement. "Why do you feel like that, Sweetheart?" I asked.

"I don't know," he said. "I just do."

At that moment, it was as if God tapped me on the shoulder and whispered, "You need to pay attention to this."

Jimmy Ray's pronouncement troubled me all evening. Our marriage was still suffering, I was still feeling neglected, and I was still battling a growing attraction to Ricky. But even though my feelings of romantic affection for Jimmy Ray had waned, I still loved him and had no desire to see him come to harm.

As I played the piano for worship that evening, then sat through the service and played again for prayer time, I was haunted by Jimmy Ray's words. They became a relentless echo in my mind.

I arrived home nearly an hour before Jimmy Ray that evening. I began to pray as I went about tidying the house, just as I had seen Mom do when I was a child at home. I went into Jimmy Ray's upstairs study to put something away. As I neared his desk, I prayed, "Oh God, why does Jimmy Ray feel like he's not going to live to be an old man? Is it Satan, trying to put fear into his heart? Or are you telling us this because we need to prepare?"

I had often heard God whisper to me through Bible passages that seemed specific to my questions or concerns. I saw Jimmy Ray's Bible lying open on his desk where he had been preparing his upcoming Easter message. So as I prayed, I looked down to see if God might reveal the answer to my question on this open page. I expected to look down and see a verse that talked about Satan being a liar and the father of all lies, or a verse that said, "Fear not." I thought surely Jimmy Ray's feelings were from Satan himself. I couldn't imagine God taking Jimmy Ray at such a young age; He was only 35 at the time. I reasoned that Jimmy Ray was much too determined and effective a minister for God to allow that kind of tragedy. And even if it were God's intention to take him at a young age, I couldn't imagine why God would share this information with me. What possible purpose could there be in my knowing in advance? I could, however, easily conceive of Satan tormenting Jimmy Ray with the fear of an early death.

No sooner had I asked God to tell me the origin of Jimmy Ray's feelings than my eyes fell on John 13:19 where Jesus predicts his own death to his disciples. There on the page, written in red, were the following words of Jesus, **"I am telling you now before it happens, so that when it does happen you will believe..."**

I felt like I had been struck between the eyes. Being drawn to this passage did not seem like a coincidence to me. It sounded like the whisper of God to which I had grown so accustom. "Oh God, when?" I asked.

"In the fall of the year," came the reply.

"In the fall of the year," I thought to myself, "the time when kids go back to school. August? Early September?"

"No. Later," came the whisper, "late September…October."

"Six months," I thought. I felt dazed, as if I had been struck on the head and couldn't think quite clearly. I struggled to get my mind around what I was hearing.

Doubts and questions began to go off like bombs exploding in my mind. Surely this could not be God. It didn't make sense. But it sounded like the whisper with which I had become so familiar. *Was* this really God? If it was, *why* would God take Jimmy Ray at such a young age? *How* would he take him? And even if it were true, why would God confide such a thing in me?

I didn't trust myself to hear clearly from God because of my ever-growing attraction to Ricky. I didn't think God would speak to someone as flawed, as unworthy as I felt I was. How could a holy God confide in someone so emotionally dead toward her spouse and consumed with thoughts of another man? I reasoned this must be Satan's attempt to torment Jimmy Ray with the dread of death, to create an even greater chasm in our marriage, and to turn my affection increasingly toward Ricky. After all, who wants to pour their heart and energy into healing a marriage that's just about to end? It's easier to invest in a new relationship with a hopeful future than it is to work on a broken one with no future. By the same token, I didn't want Jimmy Ray to die, and especially not while we were estranged. I wanted God to heal our marriage and return us to our prior state of happily ever after.

My mind continued to be pounded by doubts and questions. Was this whisper from God for the sake of our preparation or from Satan for the sake of creating a greater chasm between Jimmy Ray and myself? My mind and spirit were in torment as I wrestled with these two opposing scenarios. My thoughts went back and forth as I made a case for each scenario in my mind. I realized this message was too serious to accept on the basis of just one scripture verse. I needed more confirmation, and God was more than willing to provide it.

The first time I sought God for confirmation, he directed me to Psalm 68:5 (NIV), "A father to the fatherless, a defender of widows is God in his holy dwelling." "A passage on widows," I thought, somewhat stunned. Led by God, I turned twice more in my Bible that morning and both times my eyes fell on passages related to widows. On two more occasions, on separate days, this scenario was repeated. I asked God if this message were really from him, then opened my Bible to three random passages, and each time he pointed me to verses relaying God's love, provision, and instruction to and about widows.

Could it be true? Was I about to be widowed at the age of 34? A part of me was not surprised. I recalled how, even as a young bride in my 20's, I had a foreboding I would be a young widow. But having a foreboding about something and having God actually confirm it to you are two different things. The struggle to cope with this new revelation was agonizing. It was the kind of emotional turmoil that makes you hurt physically. I felt as though I, like the mighty oak, had just been caught in a barbed wire noose - its barbs cutting deep into my mind and heart. The more desperately I tried to dismiss or break free from the noose, the tighter and more painful it became.

At first, I tried to keep this whisper of revelation to myself. But I couldn't bear the weight of it alone. I needed prayer and counsel, so I turned to the one whom I had always turned to in a crisis – my father. I picked him up at work and we went to lunch at a little pizzeria in downtown Bloomington. There I shared with him the message I believed I had received from God.

He looked perplexed at first, and was slow to respond. But when he did, he responded with wisdom as he always had. He would not affirm that I had heard from God, nor did he dismiss the notion. He simply said, "If it's from God it will happen, and if it's not, it won't." It seemed to me a rather simplistic response, given the weight of the message, yet I knew he was right. I would simply have to wait and see how events played out before I knew for certain if the message was truly from God. But waiting would be a tiresome task. God had whispered to me that Jimmy Ray's death would come in late September or October, and it was now only April. I would have to wrestle with this revelation for at least the next six months.

As I wrestled with my thoughts that summer, I looked forward to Gal's Getaway, a weekend retreat for women who were part of our church fellowship. Our church normally sent 10 or 15 ladies to the retreat, but this summer, I was the only one registered. I felt this time away alone had been arranged by God himself. I was feeling the weight of my troubled marriage, my infatuation with Ricky, my father's declining health, and now this new whisper from God that I could barely grasp.

I longed for alone time to pray and to receive ministry. I knew if other ladies from our church went to the retreat, I would need to focus on their troubles rather than my own. But in my distressed emotional state, I didn't feel I was capable of bearing the weight of my own dilemma, much less anyone else's. Of course, there was no way I could share my burden with them. These simply were not the kinds of issues a pastor's wife shares with parishioners.

As I traveled to Gal's Getaway, I prayed God would speak to me and help me to know if this revelation of Jimmy Ray's impending death was truly from him. As familiar as the whisper sounded, I could not grasp the notion that God would reveal such a thing to me. I could not believe God would reveal such an important message to someone so flawed. How could a woman feeling so cold toward her husband and fighting affection for another man be worthy of hearing God's voice?

When I arrived at the service that night, I learned the intended speaker had been forced to cancel due to a serious illness. Another woman had been asked to take her place at the last minute.

I sat dumbfounded as I listened to this last-minute substitute share her testimony. She told about her child who suffered a serious head injury while in the care of a trusted friend. When she arrived at the hospital and saw how serious her child's injury was, she went to the hospital chapel to pray. She pleaded with God for her child's life and asked him to show her if her child would live or die. She opened up the Bible expecting words of comfort and assurance that her child would live. Instead, God directed her to a passage that confirmed the child would be taken. She too was stunned to receive a revelation from God that her loved one would die. But the child did indeed die just as God had shown her.

When the invitation for prayer was given, I bolted to the altar and began to sob. The speaker's message was yet another confirmation that the message of Jimmy Ray's impending death was truly the whisper of God. But I struggled to comprehend it.

One of the prayer counselors came over to pray with me as I knelt sobbing at the altar. I told her what I felt God had confided in me, and I also shared with her the struggle I was having with Ricky. "Nothing has happened between us," I assured her, "but I have strong feelings for him." The thought of being widowed only intensified the attraction, as I loathed the prospect of being left alone.

She was well meaning, but rather than focusing on God's guidance and strength to deal with the message of Jimmy Ray's death, she said to me, "You know this attraction is a sin and you need to ask God to forgive you of it."

"But I haven't sinned," I thought to myself as I sat speechless, stunned by the counselor's comment. My struggle was with attraction, not adultery. Perhaps she had forgotten that even our Lord was tempted, yet he did not sin. I said a prayer of repentance only to appease her, but I did not feel I had crossed the line from temptation to sin.

How I longed to be counseled by someone who had faced the same struggle. How I longed for someone to help me carry this weight. I had always depended on my father to guide me through such dilemmas in the past. But Dad's health was quickly failing, and I feared the one person I had always relied on for godly wisdom and counsel would soon be taken from me. I never felt so alone. Thankfully, God did not leave me alone in my struggle.

There's a scene in "Lord of the Rings, Return of the King" which I feel beautifully illustrates God's provision for my need of support at this time. Frodo had been charged with the task of carrying the evil Ring of Sauron into Mordor. There he was to cast the Ring into the fires of Mount Doom, thus destroying the Ring and its evil power. As Frodo and his trusted friend Sam draw closer to Mount Doom, the Ring becomes heavier and heavier around Frodo's neck. Weary from the journey and the weight of the Ring, Frodo collapses onto the ground. Sam, his faithful companion, knows what must be done. He turns to Frodo and exclaims, "I can't carry it for you, Mr. Frodo, but I *can* carry *you!*"

A determined Sam picks Frodo up from the ground and carries him ever closer to their destination.

God had entrusted me with a heavy task, the weight of which even I could not yet grasp. But he knew I could not carry the weight alone, so he put four special angels into my life to carry me as I bore the weight. Betty, Barb and Suzann were my three co-workers. They too were believers in Christ, and although they did not fully comprehend what God was doing in me, they knew of my struggles and prayed for me continuously. Ruthie was married to my father's cousin and had become a dear, dear friend. She, too, would be used by God to carry me along on the journey.

One day later that summer, as I returned to work from lunch, the weight of all I had been carrying got the better of me. I felt as if that barbed wire noose were being pulled tighter and tighter, and I was unable to cope with the intensity of the pain. As the thought of widowhood bore on my mind, Jimmy Ray and I continued to drift further and further apart. I could not bring myself to pursue closeness with him only to have him snatched away from me. The thought of being left alone caused my attraction to Ricky to slowly become an obsession. Thanks to the grace of God, I never pursued a romantic relationship with him, but I grew weary from the relentless battle to keep my emotions and behavior in check.

By this time in late summer 2001, my father was dying, and another layer of emotional pain was added. I could no longer hold back the dam of tears. I burst into Barb's office, my boss, closed the door behind me, slid down the wall into a heap on the floor, and began to sob uncontrollably. "I can't do this anymore!" I exclaimed through my tears.

Barb, moved by a motherly compassion, rolled her chair over to where I was crumpled in a heap on the floor. She patted my shoulder and attempted to console me as I sat sobbing at her feet, hot tears running down my face and onto the carpet. She and I both knew there was nothing she could do to change my situation or answer the questions that tormented me night and day. She couldn't carry the weight for me, but God had placed her in my life to carry me that day.

She, along with Betty, Suzann and Ruthie would walk a very long, dark road with me. Their non-judgmental, unconditional love and prayers would see me through to the end of my journey. Just as Frodo could not have completed his journey without Sam, I could not have completed mine without these four precious angels sent from God to carry me.

In the meantime, a member of the church had donated 10 acres of prime highway property to the church for a new worship center. Discussions regarding a new worship center got more serious, and the prospect of building was presented to the church. Jimmy Ray had spent months researching every aspect of a building project. He wanted to be sure he and the board had made informed decisions when the time came to break ground.

I was still seeking God's direction and confirmation regarding the revelation of Jimmy Ray's impending death. I wanted more of the story than God had given me. There was so much of the story he had chosen to leave out. I wanted to know *why*. I wanted to know *how*. I wanted to know *what* I was supposed to do with this revelation. And all the while I wrestled with whether this really *was* the whisper of God.

One afternoon around this time, I sat in the floor of an upstairs bedroom. With my Bible in my lap I cried out to God in desperation, "Oh God, please show me if this message about Jimmy Ray's death is really true. How could you take him when he has such a heart and passion to build a new worship center for you?"

I opened the Bible that lay in my lap and my eyes fell on I Chronicles chapter 17. In this passage, King David had determined in his heart to build a temple for God. But God sends the prophet Nathan to David with a message to the contrary. "Go and tell my servant David, 'This is what the LORD says: You are not the one to build me a house to dwell in. When your days are over and you go to be with your fathers, I will raise up your offspring to succeed you, one of your own sons, and I will establish his kingdom. He is the one who will build a house for me...'" I Chronicles 17:4, 11-12a (NIV)

As on other recent occasions I was stunned by how closely this passage related to the question I had just posed to God. God had not only confirmed Jimmy Ray's death, but he was whispering to me other vital details. First, Jimmy Ray's death would take place before he could break ground on a new worship center. Secondly, God had chosen a spiritual son to succeed him in ministry and a spiritual son to build the church he would not complete.

I wondered if God had chosen Pastor Roger Coleman to succeed Jimmy Ray. He had been on staff with us for four years by this time and seemed a logical choice. But he was still very young, and I had doubts about his preparedness to take on such a task. Following a pastor who has passed away is one of the most daunting challenges a minister can face, and I wasn't sure if the Colemans were ready for such a task at this stage in their ministry.

One would think the many confirmations God had given me would settle the matter in my mind. But I continued to plead with God for more. The guilt I felt as a result of my obsession with Ricky continually caused me to doubt both my worthiness and ability to hear from God. So I continued to ask for more and more confirmation, and God continued to provide it. One day I prayed, "Oh God, if Jimmy Ray truly is going to die, please reveal something to *him* that he will in turn share with me to confirm this message." I thought even if I were unworthy to hear God's whisper, Jimmy Ray was not. I trusted him to hear clearly from God.

Only days later, Jimmy Ray and I sat in the living room conversing over our morning coffee. He looked at me and said, "Something strange happened to me the other day." I looked at him curiously. He continued, "I was walking around the church property praying about the new worship center, and I felt like God told me I wasn't going to build the new church, just like he told David he wasn't going to build the temple."

I sat there dumbfounded. It was all I could do to conceal my amazement. Once again, God had confirmed his revelation in a way very specific to my prayer. God had taken the very scripture he directed me to only days earlier and dropped it into Jimmy Ray's heart as well. To me this was confirmation both of Jimmy Ray's impending death and the timing of it. God would certainly take him, and take him before construction on a new worship center ensued. Months earlier, Jimmy Ray had mentioned to me his desire to start on a new facility in the fall of the year. With discussions of starting a building project in the fall, and with God's message that Jimmy Ray would die in late September or October, I thought this must be confirmation that Jimmy Ray would die *that* fall, just before the church could break ground.

At the same time my father's health was declining rapidly. Dad's oncologist told him there was nothing else he could do for him. The only recommendation the doctor offered was that we call in hospice once Dad's condition deteriorated to the point our family could no longer care for him alone.

It was an excruciating summer for me emotionally. As I anticipated my husband's death, I watched my father's life slowly ebb away. By early July we could no longer care for him alone and called for the aid of hospice. He was now housebound and would be for the next several weeks.

I remember being called to my parents' house from work on more than one occasion. I would hear Mom on the other end of the line, "Lynn, the hospice nurse has been here and she thinks it's time." I would rush home as quickly as possible, hoping and praying all the way Dad would not pass before I arrived. I'm not sure why, but it seemed particularly important to me that I be holding his hand when he passed. The first couple times were false alarms. Dad would rally after the family gathered, and we would eventually return to our own homes or to work.

I stayed with my parents as often as possible to relieve Mom so she could rest or run errands. I think the most disheartening moment for me came after I had taken my father a drink of water or a bite to eat. I don't remember which for sure. After I returned to the kitchen, I heard Dad ask my mom, "Who was that lady who was just in here?"

"Well that was Lynn, Honey. That's your daughter."

"Oh. It was?" he responded. "She was so kind."

My heart felt the barbs of that noose cutting deeper as I witnessed Dad's condition deteriorate to the point he could not recognize even his own daughter. I knew his days were short. And I wondered who I would go to for counsel when he was gone. God had given me four wonderful ladies to support me, but my dad had always been the one I had gone to for godly wisdom and counsel. Dad had filled his heart and mind with

God's Word and always seemed to have just the right scripture and words of wisdom prepared for any situation.

As I watched my dad's health decline those last eight weeks of his life, I became angry with God. I could deal with Dad's death more easily than I could deal with the process of his dying. One night as I drove home from my parents' house, I cried out to God, "Why God?! Why don't you just take him?! Why do you let him suffer on and on?!"

But as I look back, I see God's hand of mercy on my father. Although his breathing was labored by cancerous tumors in his lungs, he never complained of pain. And while it pained me to witness the loss of his mental faculties, I see it now as the act of a compassionate God, allowing him to pass peacefully without the comprehension of his own demise.

On September 2, 2001, just six months after God had spoken to me of Jimmy Ray's impending death, I held my father's hand as Jesus took the other and led him safely to Heaven. I could not understand why God had taken Dad when I needed him the most. But he was safe in Jesus' arms now, and there was comfort in knowing his battle with disease was over.

With my earthly father gone, it was now time for me to lean on my Heavenly Father for strength and wisdom. God knew the perplexities I faced were beyond the wisdom of any man, and he wanted me to rely on him for comfort and counsel now.

As I stood peering down onto my father's grave, I wondered if I would soon bury my husband as well. God had given me two very specific indicators in regard to the timing of Jimmy Ray's passing. The first was that it would be in late September or October. Second, it would be before the start of a building project.

Soon after we buried my father, the worship center was put on hold due to a lack of funding, so according to that indicator, Jimmy Ray's death was not necessarily imminent. On the other hand, fall was fast approaching, and I wondered what turn of events this autumn might hold. For the next two months, I held my breath to see what, if anything would happen to Jimmy Ray.

I remember my heart pounding every time the phone rang when

Jimmy Ray was out and about, especially when making pastoral calls late in the evening or in the middle of the night. Many a night I sat at home alone in dreaded anticipation of a policeman walking up to my door bearing news of his tragic death.

But September came and September went. October came and October went. Nothing happened. Had I missed God? Had God become so displeased with me that he had allowed me to be deceived and tormented by a false message? Was this God's way of punishing me for my misplaced attraction to Ricky? I thought perhaps once autumn had passed, thoughts of Jimmy Ray's impending death would pass as well, but they didn't.

By winter I felt I had endured all I could emotionally and spiritually. I felt as if I was choking on that barbed wire noose and there was no way to break free. My health began to suffer. I contracted a bad case of bronchitis in the fall and broke out with shingles that winter. With an immune system weakened by stress, everything I contracted took longer than normal to overcome. I eventually succumbed to gastroparesis, a serious digestive condition in which the stomach muscles become paralyzed. It made eating anything more than a few bites at a time impossible and I was nauseated for hours every day. The condition would persist for years to come.

Thoughts of Jimmy Ray's death brought new challenges to ministry as well. I found it increasingly difficult to forgive parishioners who criticized or challenged Jimmy Ray. "How are they going to feel when he's dead?" I would ask myself. "They'll be sorry and ashamed when he's gone." And I wanted them to be. Although, as seen through human eyes, my feelings may have seemed justified, I knew I could not let bitterness take root in my heart. It was just one more enemy I would have to fight.

The following spring, 2002, Jimmy Ray had an out-of-town meeting, and I was left at home alone with my turmoil. I wanted to die. I thought hard about what pills might be in the house that I could use to overdose. I thought how wonderful it would be to just go to sleep and not wake up to the war zone that was raging in my mind and heart. But the question of where my spirit would wake, should I take my own life, kept me from thinking too seriously about going through with suicide.

Other times I thought about getting in my car, driving as far away as possible, and starting a completely new life – one without the weight of ministry, of grief, of a troubled marriage, of misplaced attraction and the weight of a revelation for which I could see no tangible purpose. What if God really did tell me Jimmy Ray is going to die? What was I supposed to do with that? What purpose could there possibly be in my foreknowledge of his death and the fact that God had chosen one of his spiritual sons to succeed him? I couldn't imagine having any influence on the choice of his successor. That would be a decision for the church board to make. How I longed to start a new life – one without the relentless barrage of questions for which I had no answers.

After living in this emotional and spiritual war zone for more than a year, I knew I had to share what I had been going through with Jimmy Ray. It was one of the hardest things I've ever had to do. But he knew something had been terribly wrong, and he deserved to know everything that was troubling me. And I knew opening my heart to him was the only chance our marriage had of healing.

I prayed hard about when and how I should share my emotional and spiritual battles with him. And God was faithful to guide me. One evening, after he had had a chance to eat dinner and relax a few minutes, I told Jimmy Ray I needed to talk to him. "I think I'm going to have to quit my job," I told him.

"Why?" he asked. "You love your job. And what about Betty, Barb and Suzann? You love working with them."

"I have feelings for someone at work," I said. "Neither of us has ever said or done anything inappropriate, but I have feelings for him."

"Why do you have feelings for someone else? How did that happen?" Jimmy Ray asked.

I didn't have to think about my answer. The answer was easy. "Because he was there, and you weren't," I responded. I know that was painful for Jimmy Ray to hear, but he listened carefully and made no attempt to defend himself or make excuses.

"Well I know how much you love your job and the ladies you work with," he said. "I would hate to see you give that up. You don't have to quit your job. I trust you."

I was astounded. He displayed no displeasure with me, nor did he display any malice or jealousy toward Ricky. He even encouraged me to keep my job just because he knew I loved my work and so enjoyed the friendship I shared with the ladies I worked with.

"Now, what do we need to do to fix us?" he asked. Up to this point, any attempt I had made to talk with him about our drifting relationship had been met with resistance. It had been one more stress he didn't want to deal with. In his own mind, he knew he loved me, and couldn't comprehend how neglected and resentful I had come to feel when his life got swallowed up by ministry. But when he thought he could be losing me, he was willing to make any changes necessary to repair our marriage, regardless of how those changes might be perceived by others.

One thing I always admired about Jimmy Ray was his willingness to admit a shortcoming and his commitment to making it right. From that conversation forward, Jimmy Ray became as loving and as attentive a husband a wife could ever ask for. Instead of cancelling dates with me to attend church functions, he began to carve out time for date nights. Rather than working until 8, 9, or 10:00 in the evening, he worked until 5:30 or 6. He held me often and told me he loved me many times a day, and I knew he meant it.

As difficult an emotional battle as it had been for me, God had used my attraction to Ricky to get Jimmy Ray's attention and begin the healing process in our marriage. Never again did Jimmy Ray allow me to feel neglected or taken for granted. The church would no longer be the "other woman" in our relationship. He adjusted his priorities so as to fulfill his responsibilities to the church without neglecting our marriage. "I need to remember that Jesus is married to the church, and I'm married to you," he said. He would later share that nugget of wisdom with other young ministers struggling with the same challenge.

A few weeks after I told Jimmy Ray about my feelings for Ricky, I finally shared with him the message I felt God had shared with me in regard to his death. I feared how he might react. I feared it might frighten or disconcert him, but he reacted calmly. "I don't understand it," he said, "but I'm not afraid." He had forgotten even mentioning to me that he felt he would die a young man. Evidently, God had used Jimmy Ray's brief statement just to get my attention.

It was a tremendous relief to finally share with Jimmy Ray what I believed was God's revelation to me and to know he was handling it with grace and peace. His life was in the hands of his loving, Heavenly Father, and that seemed to be all the assurance he needed. We talked openly that evening about the things I felt God had shown me. But after that initial conversation, the subject was rarely broached by either of us.

The next few years would hold more confirmation from the Lord that I had truly heard his whisper in regard to Jimmy Ray's death. And each fall of the year as the leaves turned with the changing of the seasons, my heart turned more anxious. I would wonder to myself, "Is this the fall God will take him?" Then, as the leaves fell from the trees with the approach of winter, anxiety, at least in part, fell from my heart for another year.

But I grew weary of the weight and the waiting. I felt this message of Jimmy Ray's impending death had been branded onto my heart and it would not fade, regardless of the years that passed.

One morning, several years after that initial whisper from God, I knelt by my couch praying and asking God for counsel one more time. As she had done so many times when she saw me crying in prayer, Kitty came over and nuzzled me as if to say, "What's wrong, Mommy? Are you okay?" Then she curled up and lay as close to me as she could get. Noah, while also obviously concerned, kept his vigil from the other end of the couch. Their presence was always a comfort to me when I was troubled or hurting.

"Oh God, I need an answer!" I prayed with anguish of heart. "It seems like you've shown me Jimmy Ray is going to die...but it's so hard to believe...and it's been so long. Was that message really from you?" I didn't want my husband to die, but I didn't want to dismiss a message

God may have given me for a purpose. Was it God or was I crazy? I needed to know.

As I opened up my Bible, God directed me to a passage of scripture in Habakkuk 1 and 2. And like so many times before, it provided an answer specific to my prayer. It read, "I [God] am doing something in your own day, something you wouldn't believe even if someone told you about it." That certainly seemed an appropriate response to my statement that the message was hard to believe. The passage went on to say, "Write my answer plainly on tablets..." I had told God I needed an answer and he was about to give it to me. "The vision is for a future time...If it seems slow in coming, wait patiently, for it will surely take place. It will not be delayed." There was my answer! No, I wasn't crazy. God truly had warned me of Jimmy Ray's death, but this was not God's appointed time.

Once again, God had taken the very words of my prayer and answered with a passage of scripture that spoke specifically to it. I realized now, God had not intended to take Jimmy Ray immediately. He would take him as a young man, he would take him in late September or October, and he would take him before construction on a new church commenced; but the time had not yet come. I now realized his death could be days, months or years away. God would have to teach me how to incorporate this message into my life without allowing it to consume me. I had to learn once again to trust God through pain and trust him to give me wisdom to use the foreknowledge of Jimmy Ray's death in the appropriate way at the appointed time.

With yet another confirmation of Jimmy Ray's impending death, I started trying to make as many happy memories as I could. With his 40th birthday coming up in April 2005, I thought it would provide the perfect opportunity. I called my dear friend Ruthie to confer with her.

"Ruthie, I want to do some over-the-top for Jimmy Ray's birthday. I don't know how long I'm going to have him, and I want to do something *really* special for him."

After weeks of mulling over the best way to celebrate his 40th birthday, I decided on a surprise party with a Lord of Rings theme. Jimmy Ray had become quite a fan of the movies and, although he had never been an avid reader, he had started reading the books through every year.

I put together the biggest, most elaborate party I could afford. I bought Jimmy Ray a big screen TV and commissioned a local cabinet-maker to build a custom entertainment center to house it. In order to hide the new TV and entertainment center, I took an enormous card-board box and painted Bilbo's hobbit hole on it. It completely hid Jimmy Ray's birthday gift until I was ready for him to unveil it. Then I invited a host of special guests. Besides my family and our church staff, I invited a number of out-of-town guests including George and Carol who came from Arkansas and Pastor Roger and Sharon Coleman who came from northern Indiana where they were now pastoring.

The evening was perfect. With all the special guests assembled, Jimmy Ray came home to be completely surprised by a most elaborate 40th birthday celebration. I don't think he was ever so stunned or enjoyed a celebration more than that one. And the look on his face when he found his birthday present waiting behind Bilbo's door was worth every cent.

God had been so very gracious to me. Whether Jimmy Ray lived one week, 10 weeks or 10 more years, I had been blessed with the opportunity of making the rest of our days together meaningful and sweet.

With God's help, over the next few years, I would learn to live with the barbed wire noose – this agonizing yet divine revelation. And as time would pass, like the mighty oak that enveloped the barbed wire noose that had threatened its life, the trust I placed in my Heavenly Father would envelop the barbed wire noose that had threatened mine.

CHAPTER EIGHT

NEWSONG

Part 1

It was the fall of 2006. Nearly five and a half years had passed since I heard God whisper to me that Jimmy Ray would die a young man. Not one day had passed that I did not ponder and attempt to prepare for that event. However, over time God had taught me to incorporate the message into my life without being overwhelmed by it. There were everyday tasks that needed to be seen to, and God would walk me through the completion of each one.

The past few years had brought some unexpected but welcome changes. I had resigned my position at IU and returned to school to pursue an associate degree in accounting. A prolonged struggle with gastroparesis, a partial paralysis of the stomach muscles, made it impossible for me to go to school full-time, but I was making headway. The switch from the workplace to the classroom had been a refreshing one for me. I loved the sense of accomplishment that came from learning something new. But my greatest joy, by far, was the flexibility I now had to spend more time with Jimmy Ray. Conversations over morning coffee were a treasured time for both of us. In the afternoons, he would often call to see if I wanted to run church errands with him, and I was always happy to say yes. God had performed a miracle of healing in our marriage, and as a couple, we were living happily ever after again.

Jimmy Ray had honed new skills in web and graphic design. He even started a small business called JRSCreativemedia. His only real aspiration for the business was to generate a bit of extra pocket change that we referred to as "fun money." He had a weakness for guitars and computers, and both proved expensive hobbies. We both agreed the business was a good way of generating a bit of extra income while still allowing him control over his schedule. Much to our surprise, nearly all who responded to his advertisements were young ministers involved in church planting. The business proved to be a good source of extra income, and provided Jimmy Ray valuable insight as it related to an upcoming ministry opportunity.

As was our annual custom, we made a trip to visit Jimmy Ray's parents, George and Carol that fall. And during the same trip, we enjoyed a special reunion of our RFA kids at Julie (Brummett) Lancelot's home. What a joy it was to embrace our kids once more. We hadn't seen many of them since we left them 11 years prior. Nearly all of them were now married and had children of their own, and many of them were now serving in either full-time or lay ministry. We felt like proud parents as they shared their lives and their stories with us.

We went to church with both Carol and George on Sunday. While he hadn't announced to us his newfound faith, we suspected George had come to put his faith in Christ sometime within the past three or four years. It was evident by the changes we saw in both his habits and his demeanor. This man who once had little use for church or preachers began attending church regularly as well as reading his Bible. He was reluctant to pray aloud at family functions or over dinner, but we would often hear him tell friends or family going through a crisis, "We'll sure be praying for you."

After the service, George and Carol's pastor called Jimmy Ray aside. He had a question about how our church denomination handled certain issues related to church government. But before he let Jimmy Ray go he offered this bit of information we both found comforting. He said, "Look Jim, I don't want you to ever worry about your Dad's relationship with God. I ask people at the end of nearly every service if they want to be closer to God. Your Dad raises his hand every time."

Jimmy Ray and I both rejoiced in the confirmation of what we both suspected. Happily, we would continue to see the character of Christ grow in George's life.

As we spent time driving through Northwest Arkansas that trip, we began to feel a tug in our hearts to return to the area. The population of this little corner of the state had exploded over the past several years. Growth from Wal-Mart headquarters had expanded beyond Bentonville out toward Centerton, a little town four miles due west. What had been a spot in the road in the early 1990's, had become a haven for Wal-Mart new-hires trying to escape the congestion that surrounded the corporate offices. There were few businesses in Centerton, but the cattle were moving out and families were moving in. What had once been lush, green pastures was being replaced with dozens of housing developments and apartment complexes.

"You know, I think if the opportunity ever came up to plant a church in Centerton, I'd be open to it," Jimmy Ray said.

Surprisingly, I too found myself open to the idea. There was a time I would not have given church planting a second thought. It was too uncertain. Resources were often meager, and planting pastors often had to work a second job to make ends meet. It also requires a great deal of interaction with new acquaintances. And although I had forced myself to be more open and relational, my quiet nature made forming new relationships a draining exercise for me. I simply could not see myself in a role where the health of the church was so dependent on my ability to foster new relationships.

The following spring of 2007, Jimmy Ray made another visit to Northwest Arkansas to spend a few days with his parents. I was not able to make the trip due to school commitments.

George and Carol drove Jimmy Ray to a tract of land they owned in the next town over. They had used it mainly for running cattle. Jimmy Ray was slated to inherit the land in the event of his parents' passing. As they walked around the pasture, Jimmy Ray received a welcome phone call. It was Brad McMath, one of our kids from the Rogers church (RFA), who was now pastoring in the area.

"Hey Pastor Jim!" came the voice from the other end of the line. "I've just come from a meeting of Northwest Arkansas pastors and I have to tell you about it." Jimmy Ray's ears perked up. "There are several churches in this area that want to pool resources and start a new church in Centerton. We're looking for a planting pastor, and I think *you're* the man for the job."

Brad had no idea Jimmy Ray was visiting the area when he made the call. When he found out, he was convinced the timing of Jimmy Ray's visit was God-ordained. "Pastor Jonathan Watson over at Bella Vista is heading it up. I think you should give him a call," Brad said.

Jimmy Ray's heart leapt when he heard the news. He was convinced the moment Brad delivered the news, that God had opened this door. He had a love and passion for the people of this region that had created a yearning to return. And after 12 years away from his family, he longed to return home to them as well.

"I'll tell you what, Brad, "Jimmy Ray said, "You talk to Pastor Jonathan about me. If he feels as strongly about me coming as you do, have him give me a call." Brad did just that.

Only minutes later, Jimmy Ray's phone rang once more. It was Pastor Jonathan. "Hello, this is Pastor Jonathan Watson from Bella Vista Assembly," came the voice from the other end of the line. "I've just been visiting with Brad McMath, who thinks you may be interested in joining a partnership to plant a church in Centerton. He seems convinced you're the man for the job."

"I've actually been feeling God calling Lynn and myself back to this area," Jimmy Ray responded. "I think this could be the door he's opening."

"I'd love to visit with you in person about the project sometime. Is there any time in the near future we could meet to discuss it?" Pastor Jonathan asked.

"I can be there in fifteen minutes."

Pastor Jonathan was stunned. He was pleasantly surprised to hear Jimmy Ray was in the area and was eager to meet with him. "That's perfect! I'll be looking forward to meeting you."

Jimmy Ray jumped in his pick-up and headed straight to Pastor Jonathan's church. When he arrived, Pastor Jonathan met him in the parking lot. It was a lovely day, so they stood outside as they exchanged their stories. Pastor Jonathan shared the passion God had given him to mother a church in Centerton. Both he and Jimmy Ray shared a vision for a church that would communicate God's message of love and salvation in a way that was relevant to the people of this region. And they both had a heart for the many who had uprooted themselves and their families in order to take advantage of the area's flourishing job market. They wanted to provide a safe place where people new to the area could connect with a church family and make a fresh start.

It didn't take them long to realize this was a God-ordained partnership. When they left the meeting, they knew it was only a matter of hammering out details. Both men were convinced that sometime within the next year, Jimmy Ray and I would be moving back to Northwest Arkansas to plant a new church in Centerton.

After his meeting with Pastor Jonathan, Jimmy Ray called to share the news with me. "Lynn, I have to tell you about a meeting I've just come from!" he said excitedly. I could tell from the tone in his voice he was eager to share good news. He proceeded to share with me the events of the day and how strongly he felt God had opened this door.

I was excited about the prospect too at first. My mind returned to the conversation Jimmy Ray and I had the previous fall. We had shared with each other the pull we both felt in our hearts to return to this area and had even discussed church planting in Centerton specifically. Jimmy

Ray had been hesitant to go it alone, but Pastor Jonathan's vision to plant a church as part of a partnership had lit a fire in Jimmy Ray's heart. We both felt this opportunity had been divinely arranged.

But the more I contemplated what I would be leaving behind, the more hesitant I became. It was one thing to discuss planting a church. It was quite another thing to actually do it. And the more we contemplated the move, the less enthused I became. I was happy at Ellettsville. I had everything I wanted there.

God had performed a miracle of healing in our marriage and we were happy in the life we had made for ourselves. Over time, we had been able to construct a schedule and a lifestyle at Ellettsville that allowed us the treasured times we needed to stay connected as a couple. I was doubtful church planting would afford us the same luxury and feared losing what we had worked so hard to regain.

The generous, steady income we enjoyed as well as the beautiful home God had provided, had given me the sense of financial security I longed for, as I contemplated early widowhood. That too, would have to be left behind.

I had grown to love this congregation and had carved out a role of ministry for myself that I was comfortable with. I cultivated a number of cherished friendships, and most importantly, I was near my family.

Moving to Arkansas would mean saying good-bye to so many of the people and financial resources that had given me a sense of security during an uncertain time. It meant saying good-bye to a congregation I had grown to love and felt at home with. It meant a significant cut in pay for Jimmy Ray and leaving the financial security that comes with pastoring a larger, established congregation. And of most significance to me, it meant moving away from home.

I didn't want to make the move, but I was willing as long as I knew it was truly God's desire. So I told God that if I was going to make this change, I needed him to show me clearly this is what he wanted. And He did. He whispered clearly his desire for me through the story of Ruth.

On more than one occasion, as I sat with my Bible in my lap, I prayed for God's counsel. As I opened my Bible, it repeatedly fell open to the book of Ruth, the story of a Moabite widow. It felt like déjà vu as I was reminded of the many passages about widows God pointed me to when he first shared with me the message of Jimmy Ray's death. One Saturday morning I sat flipping the remote searching for something interesting on TV. I thought about stopping on a Christian network but thought to myself, "This is Saturday. There won't be anything but children's programming on all day." Nonetheless, I felt compelled to stop on that channel. As expected, they were running children's programming that morning. But much to my surprise, they were airing a story about Ruth. It would not be the last time God would lead me to this widow's story.

As I continued to pray about the move, I continued to listen for God's whisper. I would hear it again in Sunday school one Sunday morning. The lesson that day included illustrations from the lives of three different Bible heroes and heroines. Much to my amazement, one of them just happened to be Ruth. God was whispering new insights to me all right, and I was hearing clearly. But my heart was not eager to embrace the message.

If you're unfamiliar with the story of Ruth, let me take a moment to explain the highlights. It begins with a Jewish woman named Naomi. She, along with her husband and two sons, moved from Israel to Moab during a famine in search of food.

Soon after they moved to Moab, Naomi's husband died. She was left with her two sons who married Moabite women. Her daughters-in-law were Ruth and Orpah. Less than ten years into their marriages, both Ruth and Orpah were also widowed. Now all three women, Naomi, Ruth and Orpah were left without husbands or children. How would they survive?

Naomi made the decision to return to Israel in hope of finding help and provision among her own people. Ruth and Orpah started the journey with her, but Naomi tried hard to dissuade them. She knew she had nothing to offer them, and pleaded with them to return to their families where they would be provided for. But Ruth insisted on returning with Naomi to the land where Ruth's late husband, Naomi's son, had been born and raised. Ruth clung to her mother-in-law declaring, "Your people will be my people and your God my God." Ruth left her own home and family and bound herself to Naomi, while Orpah turned back to Moab.

God was gracious to Ruth and blessed her in the land of Israel. He had gone ahead of her and made provision for her every need. Although Ruth's Moabite roots made her the likely object of prejudice in Israel, she found financial provision there. But that's not all. Ruth also found love and protection, as well as financial provision, in the arms of a new husband, Boaz. Ruth's unselfish decision to leave the security of her own home and family for the sake of her mother-in-law was rewarded with both provision and love.

By leading me time and time again to this story of Ruth, God was revealing my own future to me. He was showing me that I was being called away from my own home and family, just like Ruth. It was his desire that I return to the place where my husband had been born and raised and that I should bind myself to his family, and to his mother in particular, just like Ruth. In fact, as we sat discussing our move over coffee one morning I told Jimmy Ray, "I think part of my calling back to Northwest Arkansas is to be a blessing to your mother." His eyes filled with tears as he was deeply moved by my desire to be a source of joy in his mother's life.

I felt certain God was also showing me that I would be widowed in the place of my husband's birth. Even though I was leaving behind what I considered essential financial security, I was confident God would make provision for me there, just like he had for Ruth. And God comforted me in this: he would not leave me in my loneliness, but he would have a Boaz waiting for me, just as he had for Ruth.

With solid confirmation and the assurances God had given me of continued provision, I agreed to make the move back to Northwest Arkansas. In August 2007, Jimmy Ray made the call to Pastor Jonathan informing him of our firm decision to accept the church planting position.

I immediately began to feel the ache of leaving beloved friends and family. I dreaded moving into a ministry where I had no established relationships. Financial concerns began to weigh on my mind as well, as Jimmy Ray would be required to take a significant cut in pay. I knew this new endeavor would require more of my time and energy than any previous ministry, and I worried I might have difficulty finding part-time work. Full-time work was plentiful, but I was still struggling with gastroparesis, and feared I would not have the physical stamina to take on both full-time work and church planting activities.

It would be another five months before we made the move from Ellettsville to Northwest Arkansas. During that time, we saw God's plan of provision unfold before us. Before bringing us in, the church planting committee made sure they had enough money in reserve to pay us a salary for at least one year. Several of the churches agreed to continue supporting the new church for an additional year to help with start-up expenses.

Jimmy Ray's parents opened their home to us and our two beloved cats, Kitty and Noah, for as long as we needed. We had a home to sell and a hefty mortgage payment to go with it, so the provision of free housing was a tremendous relief. In short, the largest part of our first year's expenses was provided for before we ever said good-bye to our church in Ellettsville.

God was faithful in other ways as well. As news of our return to Northwest Arkansas spread, we began to receive calls from our kids who still lived in the area. Many of the young people we had ministered to at RFA over a decade earlier, were either still living in or had returned to the area. The first call we received was from our "first boy," C.J. Brummett. As a youth, C.J. had been Jimmy Ray's greatest antagonist. As an adult, he would become his greatest advocate.

C.J. and his lovely wife Jen, along with their new twin boys, were attending RFA at the time. They loved the congregation there, and C.J. in particular felt a strong connection to the church where he had grown up in the pastor's home. But God had begun to stir their hearts toward a new mission. They were open to that new mission, but were unclear about what form it might take. When they heard Jimmy Ray was coming to plant a new church, they knew in their hearts this was it. They felt God drawing them to be part of the new church, and committed themselves to doing whatever was necessary to see this new church birthed.

Annette, our "first girl," was next to call us. She and her family were attending Pastor Jonathan's church. Pastor Jonathan had announced one Sunday evening that a pastor had been chosen for the new Centerton church. And although he hadn't given his name, Annette derived from Pastor Jonathan's description of Jimmy Ray, that it must be him. As soon as she arrived home, she called to see if it were true. "Hey, Jimmy Ray?" inquired an excited voice on the other end. "I just got home from church and Pastor Jonathan said a guy from Indiana who used to be a youth pastor in this area is coming to be the new pastor at Centerton. Is it you?" she asked. "Is it you?!" Jimmy Ray confirmed her suspicion.

As word of our soon return spread, we continued to receive calls from others of our kids in the area. Jimmy Ray received calls from more than one of them desiring to work on his staff. He would have loved to hire each and every one of them, but there simply was no room in the budget for additional paid staff.

The calls we received from our kids over the next several weeks were a tremendous boost to my spirit and created a sense of excitement that, up to that point, had been missing. I was now excited about the prospect of working side by side with those we had mentored over a decade earlier. I was also eager to reach out to those of our kids, who as adults, had become disconnected from God or their church family. I so wanted to help them find their way back to his love and protection.

It was nearing time for us to say good-bye to Ellettsville and move into our new ministry. It was probably late November or sometime into December 2007. Jimmy Ray was certain we had been called by God to reach out to the people of Centerton and the greater Northwest Arkansas region. But he desired clearer, more focused direction from God about the demographic we were to reach.

Every Wednesday morning he gathered with his Ellettsville staff for a time of prayer for the church and for that evening's service. It was during one such prayer gathering that God gave him the focus he had been praying for.

As Jimmy Ray circled the sanctuary praying, asking for greater focus, God gave him a vision. He had never had a vision like it before, nor would he ever have another. His surroundings faded and he saw with his eyes a sea of teenagers. They had their hands raised to God, worshiping him. But he knew what he was witnessing was a scene from the past. God then opened his eyes to see these same people at present. They were now adults disconnected from God and from his church. They did not hate God; life had simply happened to them and they found themselves away from him. Many had walked away when people within their church hurt them. Others left when they made a poor life decision and were too ashamed to return. Still others had become disconnected when they relocated for the sake of a job and simply had not found a church that felt like home and family to them.

Jimmy Ray looked among the sea of faces to see if any were familiar. He recognized only one. It was Melissa. She was one of our kids from RFA - a faithful member of the youth group who had devotedly expressed a desire for God. We had seen her grow and mature spiritually under our ministry at RFA, and she continued to serve God after we left.

But like the many others Jimmy Ray saw in his vision, Melissa had become the victim of life and its many unseen dangers. A divorce and the strained relationships that followed, found her disconnected from both her church family and from God. Our hearts had been broken for her when we heard the news. Perhaps God would use us to help this lost sheep find her way back into the safety of his loving arms.

Jimmy Ray realized now to whom he was being sent. He was being sent to reach God's lost sheep. God was calling us to leave the ninety and nine to go after the one, of whom Jesus had spoken in Matthew 18. As he shared his vision with me, I began to develop a greater passion for our new work. God was giving me the grace I needed to say good-bye to one life and the passion I needed to embrace another.

Now that God had brought his mission for the new church clearly into focus, there was one more detail for which we needed God's guidance. What should the new church be named? We prayed about and pondered a number of different possibilities; Cross Point? Genesis? New Life? But none of them sounded right. Then one afternoon, as he was in his study, Jimmy Ray was inspired with the name of the new church. It not only described one very important aspect of our ministry, but also described the mission God had so clearly revealed to us. It described the hope we felt for every lost sheep to whom we were being sent. The church would be called Newsong.

I could not think of a more fitting name for the new church. When I considered Jimmy Ray's passion for helping people connect with God through worship and our desire to see those who had lost their song when they walked away from Christ gain it back again, it became apparent how beautifully the name Newsong reflected the heart of our new mission.

While God was bringing into focus future aspects of our ministry for Jimmy Ray, he was bringing into focus aspects of our personal life for me. Over the course of the past seven years, as I had prayed for confirmation and guidance in regard to Jimmy Ray's eventual passing, God had led me numerous times to Psalm 37. But on every occasion I had struggled to understand the connection between this passage and the message God had whispered to me regarding our future.

As I sat on my couch once again seeking God's counsel in regard to the message of Jimmy Ray's death and how it might relate to our move, my Bible once again fell open to Psalm 37. As I read through the passage, I was stunned by the message that leapt from the page. The chapter was peppered with verses regarding the possession and occupation of land. Seven different times, reference is made to inheriting or occupying land. Those verses captured my attention as though they were flashing neon signs. Why had I not seen this before?

I now saw that the possession of land was to be a key component in both our personal lives and our mission. Details regarding just how integral the possession and occupation of land would become will be explained as the story unfolds.

Part 2

On February 2, 2008, Jimmy Ray and I loaded up a trailer along with Kitty and Noah, and moved to Northwest Arkansas. We arrived at George and Carol's around 11:00 p.m. They gave us a loving and warm welcome reminiscent of the one they had given us 22 years earlier when I had come with Jimmy Ray for my first visit. As always, Carol wanted to know if we were hungry and what she could fix us to eat. It was a welcome reception after a long journey.

The following weeks were filled with activity. After settling in at the house came the usual business that needs tending when you move from one state to another. Plus for me there was the inevitable job search. I had just completed my associate degree in accounting the previous December and began a diligent search for a part-time accounting position. But as I had feared, there were few part-time jobs available. Part-time jobs were plentiful in Fayetteville, nearly 35 miles away. But with gas nearing $4 a gallon, it was simply too far to make the commute worthwhile. Jobs closer were either full-time, required a bachelor's degree, or were outside my field. I soon realized I would have to compromise. As much as I hated the thought of full-time work during this crucial start-up period, I applied for a handful of full-time jobs for which I thought I might be well suited. I wondered if perhaps God had ordained full-time work for me because he knew I would soon be widowed and called upon to support myself financially.

The first job offered to me was a position at John Brown University (JBU). JBU is a Christian university just minutes from where we were living with Jimmy Ray's parents. And while I was not enthused about full-time work, I was excited about working at a Christian university. I found the supervisor, her boss, and the other gentleman who interviewed me to be open and friendly. I felt my personality melded well with theirs, and I looked forward to a positive work experience.

Ironically, I had heard from a mutual friend several years earlier that Jimbo had been offered a professorship at JBU and was teaching in their

Bible department. The same friend also told me Jimbo had never married. It didn't really surprise me. I could easily imagine him being so focused on education and career that he let the prospect of marriage simply pass him by, which apparently was the case.

I looked forward to perhaps running into Jimbo. His life had been an eclectic one to say the least, and I was curious to know how Jimbo the professor contrasted with Jimbo the student whom I had known a quarter of a century earlier. After leaving IU, he went on to earn a law degree, a master's degree in theological studies, a Ph.D. in religious studies, live in seven different states, teach overseas, and make at least one major career change. Considering the diverse lives we had both lived, I thought it uncanny we should find ourselves employed by the same small school in the same small town nearly 600 miles from where we first met.

A week or two after I started work at JBU, I asked Jimmy Ray if he wanted me to track down Jimbo to see if he were aware of any Bible students interested in gaining some practical ministry experience. Perhaps he would know of a student looking to do an internship that might want to help us at Newsong. This was the time of year a senior ministry major might be looking for those kinds of opportunities. And quite frankly we were desperate for workers. We needed help in every area from the safety team to sound technicians and drummer to door greeters. We were confident God would connect us with the essential team members once we arrived. Jimmy Ray was excited about the prospect of making some of those connections through JBU, and asked me to contact Jimbo.

It was easy enough to find Jimbo's class schedule posted on the school's web site. I reasoned the best time to catch him would be between his 11:00 class and lunch. So sometime around noon, I walked over to his building, found the classroom I believed to be his, and waited for the professor inside to finish his lecture.

But as I peered through the window, I questioned whether I had found the right room. The professor inside looked very different from the Jimbo I had said good-bye to 25 years prior. So to be certain, I stopped one of the female students as she was exiting the classroom. "Is this Blankenship's class?" I asked.

"Yes, it is," she replied with a smile.

The bronze tan he had once earned during his days as a lifeguard had faded. His once dark brown hair had turned silver gray, and he wore a full silver beard to match. His athletic build had given way to a physique more common to a man nearing 50, and he had traded in his contacts for a pair of dark-rimmed reading glasses, which sat on the tip of his nose. I expected him to look older, but I hadn't anticipated difficulty in recognizing him. Time has a way of transforming all of us, though, as I was about to discover.

I stepped into the classroom between exiting students and stood patiently by the door while Jimbo gathered his lecture notes. I was sure he would recognize me immediately, so I broke the 25-year silence with an attempt at humor. "Boy, they'll let just about *anybody* teach here, won't they?" I waited for a chuckle and cordial response. I knew he would be surprised to see me. I had hoped the surprise would be a pleasant one.

Jimbo cocked his head toward the door to see who was speaking and responded without a change in facial expression, "Apparent-*ly*," with a heavy emphasis on the "*ly*".

"Do you have a couple minutes?" I asked.

"Yeah. Let's go down to my office." There was still no smile or warmth of expression. His cool demeanor surprised me.

He walked passed me through the door and walked briskly down the hallway, staying about three paces in front of me. About half way down the hallway, without breaking stride, he turned and looked at me quizzically and asked, "Do I *know* you?"

I was stunned he hadn't recognized me. Apparently, time had changed my appearance as much as it had his. "You're kidding, right?" I responded.

As soon as I responded, he realized who I was. I think he was a bit embarrassed for not having recognized me right off. But he had been taken unaware and vision issues made it difficult for him to clearly make out facial features at times. When we got to his office he offered me a seat and took his behind the desk.

"I'm actually here to ask for your help," I said. "My husband and I have moved back to this area to start a new church in Centerton, and we're looking for workers." I took out a small stack of business cards and half-page posters and laid them on his desk. "I was wondering if you had any students you think might be interested in helping us out."

He seemed happy enough to take the materials I offered, and said he would see what he could do. We chatted for just a few minutes, catching up on the latest family news and the different places life had taken us. We found our lives had taken very different paths. I, of course, had married just out of college and had spent the past 21 years in ministry alongside my husband. Jimbo had remained single, having chosen to devote his energies to education and career.

Our conversation was brief, as he had a meeting to attend. I saw him on occasion in the cafeteria, but only long enough to smile and nod or offer a brief, "Hello." What brief encounters we did have made me aware of the distance not only geography, but time itself had put between us. He seemed more like a stranger to me than an old acquaintance.

Although I had been hopeful about making a positive contribution to JBU, I found those first few days and weeks surprisingly difficult. I was not as well suited for the position as I had originally anticipated, and was surprised by the scope of responsibilities. It seemed everything that could go wrong did go wrong those first couple weeks, and every day felt like trudging through quicksand. Regardless of the effort I exerted, I seemed to fall further and further behind. I went home each night completely exhausted, in part because of the job stress, and in part because I was still struggling with gastroparesis, and eating enough to maintain sufficient stamina was a challenge.

I began to pray about whether to stay on or to quit while the department might still have another candidate waiting in the wings. I made my decision after an unfortunate misunderstanding over a day I took off for family business. I was called into the boss's office the next morning where he expressed his displeasure that I had not come in the previous day. I sat there both dumbfounded and disheartened. I had gotten approval to be off, mentioning my need to be out for the day as early as my first interview. But he evidently had forgotten and thought

I had simply skipped work. He said he was willing to chalk it up to a simple misunderstanding, but for me it was the proverbial straw that broke the camel's back. I could handle a certain amount of work stress, but I could not bear being seen as a problem employee. I gave my notice the next morning, agreeing to stay as long as needed for them to fill the position and to train the next person. My career at JBU lasted a disappointing three and a half weeks.

As I look back on the experience, I believe the way events unfolded at JBU were all a part of God's design. My short stint at JBU helped us get through what otherwise would have been a financial shortfall. But more importantly, it made me aware of how desperately I was needed by Jimmy Ray during this crucial start-up phase of the church. I would not regret my decision to resign when I did.

On May 18, 2008, in the cafeteria of Centerton Gamble Elementary School, Newsong Church was officially launched. There were 40 people in attendance. Over the past three and a half months since our move, we had watched God provide everything from personnel to a meeting place and from a cargo trailer to a truck to pull it.

Because we would be meeting in a school, we needed a solution for storing and transporting our equipment and Kids' Church supplies. The

Jimmy Ray and George in front of the new truck – Summer, 2008

Severns' church agreed to let us borrow their cargo trailer for as long as we needed. It was an answer to prayer, but we still had no way of pulling the trailer. Jimmy Ray's pickup truck was 14 years old by this time and not nearly hefty enough to pull a heavy trailer. But God intervened.

As Jimmy Ray sat working in his parents' upstairs bedroom that was serving as both our living quarters and church office, George called up to him from downstairs, "Son!"

"Yeah, Dad," Jimmy Ray answered as he walked to the top of the stairs.

"We need to go down and get you a pickup that can pull that trailer," George said.

"Well, I'd love that Dad, but we just can't afford any extra payments right now," Jimmy Ray responded.

"Well, there's no need to worry about that. You just go down and pick out what you need and I'll take care of it," George said.

We both gasped with surprise. After the generosity George and Carol had shown us by opening their home to our two cats and us, we could not and did not expect anything more. But George and Carol, like so many parents, derived great joy in making sure their kids had whatever they needed, and it made George smile to do it.

That afternoon, George and Jimmy Ray went down to a little car lot not more than half a mile down the road. There they found a beautiful, red, four-door, four-wheel drive pickup with a towing package. It was only one year old, and was everything we needed. Not only was it hefty enough to pull the trailer, but also the back seating space gave us plenty of room for more fragile items like Jimmy Ray's guitars and a television for Kids' Church. God had not only provided, he had provided in perfect detail.

When I look back at pictures we took of Jimmy Ray and his dad with the truck that day, it's hard to tell who was more proud of that pick-up – George or Jimmy Ray.

Our next greatest logistical concern was a sound system. One Sunday morning after sharing Newsong's vision at Pastor Jonathan's church, Mark Kendall, Bella Vista Assembly's drummer, approached Jimmy Ray.

"Hey, I don't know if you can use it or not, but I have an entire sound system in my basement I'm not using. Newsong is welcome to use it as long as they need it," Mark said. Jimmy Ray was surprised, and yet not surprised by God's provision. Mark went on to say, "My wife, Mary and I have been involved in worship ministry, too, and if you can use us, we'd love to be part of your worship team."

Mark and Mary were a tremendous blessing, and we were delighted to have them as part of our team. Once again, God had provided in perfect detail.

Frankie, one of our girls from RFA, along with C.J.'s wife, Jen, oversaw our Kids' Church and nursery. Others who had joined us from Bella Vista Assembly, our mothering church, assisted them. C.J. and Frankie's husband Theo helped with set up, oversaw safety, and made sure everyone who came was greeted with a warm smile and a friendly handshake.

What a tremendous joy it was to have two of our kids and their families, as well as the many others like Mark and Mary whom God had sent to partner with us in this new ministry. And on Newsong's first Sunday morning, it was a special joy to see Melissa's face, the only one Jimmy Ray had recognized in his vision. She worked third shift on Saturday nights, so we knew it required a significant effort on her part to be there. It honored us to see her.

Jimmy Ray spent the first five months instilling into our core group God's vision for Newsong Church and striving to create relational bonds within the church family. He felt it was essential to build a strong spiritual and relational foundation before doing a community-wide push. By October of that year he felt it was time to introduce Newsong Church to the whole of Centerton.

We introduced ourselves to the community and invited one and all to join Newsong Church for her grand opening on October 5, 2008. It was an exciting day marked by an atmosphere of celebration, which Jimmy Ray had created with intent. The platform had been decorated with towering, multicolored balloon bouquets as well as brightly colored banners he designed himself. We planned not only an inspirational service, but also a fun-filled afternoon for all who came. The church provided free hamburgers and hot dogs for lunch, and there was a huge blow-up obstacle course, complete with bounce house and slide in the gym for the kids. Every person who came received a cup adorned with the Newsong logo and filled with an assortment of candy and other goodies. The day was filled with joy, excitement, and most importantly God's blessing.

Newsong's grand opening generated its largest attendance yet. There were upwards of 200 in attendance that day. Of course, many were family members and well-wishers who normally attended other churches, but many others were the lost and disconnected sheep God had called us to. I remember a conversation with one man in particular. He and his family of nine had visited a number of churches over the past several years trying to find a "home." They had all grown so weary of the search; they had all but resolved to quit looking. But when they heard a church in the area was having a "grand opening", they thought it such a peculiar idea they just had to check it out. Fortunately, they found what they were looking for at Newsong and their family became a faithful part of the church.

With Newsong up and running and all of her immediate needs met, Jimmy Ray and I were able to turn our attention more fully on completing a personal project. Our house in Ellettsville had been on the market for seven months before it sold in late August. With the house sold and a good deal of equity in our pockets, it was now time to decide what we would do for permanent housing. We had two choices. We could buy an existing home in Centerton, close to our mission field. Or, if we chose, George and Carol were willing to sign over a portion of some pastureland they owned on which we could build a home.

When the choice presented itself, I knew in my heart the choice God was leading us to make. God had shown me before we left Ellettsville he had land prepared for us here. And while buying a home in Centerton may have seemed a more convenient, perhaps even more logical choice, I was convinced it was God's desire we accept the Severns' offer of land and build a home in the country.

Jimmy Ray's parents owned a tract of land just minutes from Centerton. It was primarily a field used for running cattle – the same field in which Jimmy Ray had been standing when he got the call from Brad about the church plant. George and Carol graciously signed over two and a half acres to Jimmy Ray and me on which to build our home. It was a dream-come-true for both of us. Jimmy Ray had long desired to have a home in the country. I had always dreamed of a home on top of a hill overlooking a pond, and that's exactly what we got. But more amazing to me still, was the fact that God's promise to provide us with land had come to pass.

Because finances were still somewhat limited, we decided to take the equity from our home and build an oversized garage with a studio apartment above. That way, we would be free of house payments while we saved for a more permanent home.

Carol and Jimmy Ray at the start of barn construction
Early fall, 2008

We chose a plan that looked like a barn and would paint it red because we thought it fit perfectly into the landscape. And although it was really a home, it will forever be referred to as "the barn."

As we began to make significant headway on the barn, Newsong was seeing significant growth. By the end of 2008, only seven months after her birth, Newsong was averaging around 90 in attendance, a good showing for a new church in a small community.

The Arkansas Assemblies of God district officials took notice and were pleased with the growth Newsong was enjoying. Jimmy Ray informed Rev. Larry Moore the District Superintendent that a tract of land immediately adjacent to the school where we were holding services had come up for sale. It was Jimmy Ray's hope the district council would purchase the land for the church.

In the spring of 2009, Rev. Moore extended an invitation to Jimmy Ray and me to present a land purchase proposal to the district committee. Jimmy Ray compiled an impressive proposal complete with financial details and photos of the property, and we headed down to Little Rock to present it.

When it was time for Jimmy Ray to make his presentation, we were ushered into a room where the committee had been meeting to discuss a myriad of other business. It was an intimidating venue with an impressive boardroom where a dozen or so middle-aged men in dark suits sat in oversized black leather chairs around a large, dark, wooden conference table. They were serious about the business at hand, and their facial expressions were proof of it.

After the appropriate introductions were made, Jimmy Ray was invited to commence his proposal that the district council purchase five acres adjacent to Gamble Elementary School where Newsong had been meeting. He was well prepared and well spoken; his presentation took all of about ten minutes. After he finished, we were ushered out of the room and directed down a long hallway where we were to wait while the committee discussed the proposal.

We were asking the district council to invest close to $90,000, and were certain there would be much discussion. But much to our surprise, only about five minutes later one of the committee members asked us to return to the boardroom.

As we entered the room, we started toward what had been our two seats. But Rev. Moore stopped us at the door and said, "No, that's alright. You don't need to sit down." We wondered if the lack of discussion would prove good news or ill. "We just want you to know that we've accepted your proposal, and we've approved the purchase of five acres next to the school."

We were dumbfounded. We could scarcely believe our proposal had been accepted so quickly, but we believed it was truly the favor of God and were thankful to both him and the district committee.

"Thank you so much, Rev. Moore," Jimmy Ray said with heartfelt gratitude. "We can't express how grateful we are for this."

As we walked down the hallway to exit the building, Jimmy Ray and I looked at each other in amazement. It felt as though we were living in a dream. Church planting, the one ministry I had feared the most because of its unique challenges was proving to be the most exciting and rewarding ministry I had ever been allowed by God to be part of. As obstacles arose, we watched as God overcame each one in some miraculous manner. It was also exciting for me to see God's promise of land being fulfilled for Newsong as well as for Jimmy Ray and me personally.

With the committee's approval to purchase the land, all that remained were the legal aspects of the purchase. Jimmy Ray immediately saw to having the land surveyed and went to work on a purchase agreement to present to the landowner. As Jimmy Ray was working with the district on the land purchase, we were wrapping up work on the barn. The project took longer than expected, as all construction projects do. But Jimmy Ray, George, and I along with a long list of other volunteers worked diligently to see the project through to completion. When it was finished, we had a lovely little home in the country, completely paid for. We moved into our little red barn on April 1, 2009, just 16 days before Jimmy Ray's 44th birthday. And what a birthday present it was!

CHAPTER NINE

A MYSTERIOUS ILLNESS

Spring and summer of 2009 were proving to be beautiful seasons at the barn. It rained just enough to turn our yard and surrounding pastures a lush, dark green, but the sun was a much more frequent visitor than the rain. The bright mornings made you want to jump out of bed and get coffee brewing early.

Jimmy Ray loved our new little home in the country, and looked for any excuse to jump on the new tractor he had gone halves on with his dad. Building a home in the middle of a pasture meant keeping up with a rough, thick lawn and lots of it. The only way we had to keep a handle on it was to mow it with the bush hog, and Jimmy Ray could find no other way he would rather pass the time. There was never a happier, more contented expression on his face than when he was dressed in his overalls and ball cap pulling the bush hog behind his new Kubota tractor. Although we had no aspirations of becoming farmers ourselves, we enjoyed the wildlife from our new vantage point. Waking up to the sound of birds and the scene of grazing cattle out our large front picture window was a relaxing way to start the day. Every now and then we were treated with the sight of deer wandering the pastures that surrounded the barn. On one particular afternoon I spied nearly 30 deer as they wandered out from the back woods across the adjacent pasture and down toward the road. We never lost our awe of the beauty with which God had surrounded us.

Living with nature, however, can bring a few unsolicited adventures as well. More than one field mouse would confuse our barn for a hotel and my pillow for their bed. I'm afraid, however, they often found "service with a smile" meant the smile of a cat as they hung dangling from the mouth of either Kitty or Noah. Although the cats had never seen a mouse before the barn, these hunters found mousing an inherent skill. Word must have quickly spread throughout the field mice population that the big red barn was an unfriendly place to visit, or else we finally got the access points sufficiently plugged, because the barn doesn't get nearly as many little hairy visitors as it once did.

It was sometime around the middle of June - less than three months after we moved into the barn. Jimmy Ray had come inside to shower after spending the morning working outdoors. He drew my attention to a rash forming on his arms and torso that we assumed was an allergic reaction to the grass or a weed he had encountered while tending the yard. After several weeks with no improvement, the rash was examined and biopsied by a dermatologist who diagnosed it as a harmless condition that would eventually resolve on its own. The rash, however, persisted. But believing it to be a benign condition, Jimmy Ray pursued it no further. He was too busy pastoring a new, growing church and making sure he had everything in order before he presented a purchase agreement to the owners of the property adjacent to the school. We would find out months later the rash was a symptom of a much more serious condition.

On July 2, 2009, we made a visit to the home of Charles and Louis White, owners of the five acres Newsong was interested in buying. We presented them with the purchase agreement which they happily signed.

As we left the Whites' home, Jimmy Ray commented that he didn't feel well. Putting his palm on his forehead he remarked that he might have a fever. A quick check with the thermometer after we got home confirmed his suspicion. He did have a low-grade fever. Not being one to succumb quickly to a light bug though, he persevered through the weekend. He oversaw setup at the school on Saturday and then led worship, preached, and oversaw tear down on Sunday. Then Sunday afternoon we met at Julie (Brummett) Lancelot's house for a visit with a few of our kids from RFA. It was a full weekend for someone feeling under the weather.

When the next Wednesday rolled around Jimmy Ray was still feeling ill, so I offered to take the Wednesday night service for him. Although I don't consider the more up-front ministries my forte, I had led worship and spoken enough times to muddle through. As always, God made up for whatever talent I lacked for preaching, and the service proceeded smoothly that evening.

After a barrage of blood tests for tick-borne diseases and other infections, Jimmy Ray was presented with what seemed an obvious diagnosis of mononucleosis (mono). His Epstein-Barr Virus (EBV) count, used to detect mono, was 750+. A count of 22 is considered high enough to diagnose mono. The doctor told Jimmy Ray he had the worst case of mono he had ever seen. Unfortunately, there is no cure for mono, and it often takes weeks or even months to resolve on its own. As severe as his case was, Jimmy Ray was looking at a possible three to six month recovery.

By the time August rolled around, Jimmy Ray was house bound, so I began to oversee all the church services. I led worship and preached most Sundays and Wednesday nights and scheduled speakers for the services I couldn't oversee. Having been one to avoid center stage in the past, I felt ill equipped for these new responsibilities, but I was willing to do whatever was necessary to keep the church running until Jimmy

Ray recovered. I feared, however, that the health of our baby church would suffer in the absence of their shepherd and prayed fervently that Jimmy Ray would soon be able to return to his duties. I didn't want the church he had worked so diligently to establish dwindle under my inferior leadership.

As I thought back over the events of July, it occurred to me that Jimmy Ray first felt ill the day the purchase agreement for the land had been signed. God began to whisper to me that Jimmy Ray's illness was somehow connected to Newsong's land purchase and that the answer to his illness would come once the closing papers were signed. I shared this with Jimmy Ray, and we both latched onto that hope. But Jimmy Ray's condition continued to worsen.

I took over the legwork and phone conversations to oversee the land closing for Jimmy Ray. A certain amount of coordination had to happen between Newsong Church, the Arkansas District, the landowners, the surveyor's office, the City Council and the title company. Because of Jimmy Ray's weakened condition, it was agreed our sectional Presbyter, Rev. Gary Wheat, and a representative from the District Office would sign the closing papers in his stead.

Jimmy Ray's fevers continued to get higher and were now recurring on a daily basis. He often called to me in the night seeking relief from the ever-rising fevers. Night after night I would get cold, wet towels to lay on his arms, legs, and forehead to cool him down and provide some relief from the heat of the fevers.

Jimmy Ray's condition worsened with the onset of excruciating headaches. They were reminiscent of the ones he endured during his early years at Ellettsville. The pain was almost unbearable at times, and I rushed him to the ER on more than one occasion in a desperate search for relief.

On one such night, he was writhing in pain, holding his head as I rushed him to the hospital. I made the comment that we needed to ask Jesus to help him. He snapped at me with a desperate, frustrated tone. "If Jesus wanted to help me, he would heal my head!" But as quickly as the words left his lips, he felt sorry for doubting his Lord and began to repent,

"I'm sorry, Jesus. I know you want to help me. I'm sorry, Jesus." Despite the severity of the pain, he was careful not to accuse his Lord of neglect or wrongdoing.

Over the next several weeks I endeavored to care for Jimmy Ray at home. But rather than improving, his condition continued to deteriorate. His fevers continued to climb while his strength waned. I realized he was in need of more professional attention than I could provide. So I sought assistance from his physician.

Jimmy Ray's doctor admitted him to the Intensive Care Unit (ICU) of the local hospital so his case could be reviewed and I could get some much-needed rest. A review of his blood work set up concerns he might have lymphoma, a type of cancer. However, every test came back negative. There was no sign of cancer anywhere in his body. Having no new diagnosis, the hospital sent Jimmy Ray home where they assumed he would eventually recover from a very serious case of mono.

Only days after returning home, Jimmy Ray began experiencing new symptoms. One evening as we sat watching television, a surge of searing nerve pain went through his shoulder like a bolt of lightning. "A-a-u-u-g-gh!" he cried out as he bolted out of his seat and grabbed his shoulder in an attempt to ease the pain. It was almost more than he could bear. A quick examination around his shoulder blade revealed a small red sore. Having had shingles myself several years earlier, I feared he had been smitten with the same condition.

He eventually lay down for the night, still in terrible pain. My heart was in anguish as I sat helplessly by, witness to his suffering. "Let me pray for you, Sweetheart," I said and then proceeded to plead with God to give him relief.

In that moment I was not concerned with diagnoses or remedies. All I wanted was for God to intervene in that moment to give this man I loved a few minutes of rest from his agony. Thankfully in his mercy, God heard and answered. Only minutes later, Jimmy Ray lay sleeping peacefully, free from pain for the moment. And while the underlying condition remained, God had granted him a moment's rest, perhaps like he gives a mother rest between the pains of childbirth.

I had often heard my mother describe the anguish of childbirth as she reminisced of the birth of my brother and me. I cringed as she relayed the unpleasantness of the experience. But she would always add without fail, "…but God made it so you can rest between the pains."

Rest between the pains. That's what I was witnessing. God had seen Jimmy Ray at his limit, and he had allowed him this brief respite between the pains. I breathed a sigh of momentary relief as I watched Jimmy Ray rest quietly throughout the evening.

Unfortunately the rest would not last long. As the nerve pain dissipated, a new condition presented itself. Sometime in late August, about seven weeks into his illness, Jimmy Ray began experiencing blurred and double vision. Reading, watching television, or using his computer, the only things he had to pass the time while he was sick, became increasingly difficult. Eventually, he couldn't make out anything clearly with or without the aid of glasses. For him, this was perhaps the most disheartening part of his illness. Not only had he lost the ability to enjoy his only pastimes, but also there is something about the inability to see that makes one feel intensely insecure.

Depression started to take hold. Up to this point he had faced his illness as bravely as anyone could have. But to have his vision impaired to the point of near blindness was simply overwhelming.

"You're going to get your answer as soon as the closing papers on the church property are signed," I reassured him. It seemed to give him hope as he realized how strongly I felt about the connection between Newsong's land purchase and a resolution to his illness. He too began to cling to the hope he would see an end to his illness on the day Newsong closed on the land.

For all our frustration and desperation in regard to his compounding illness, God was gracious in this; he had surrounded us with a church family who became a constant source of encouragement and strength. They continually expressed their love and concern and regularly sent uplifting Facebook messages and cards riddled with scriptures of hope and peace.

CJ organized a special prayer meeting to be held at the barn. If Jimmy Ray couldn't get to Newsong, Newsong would come to Jimmy Ray. One evening in late August, about an hour before dusk Jimmy Ray and I sat waiting and watching out our picture window to see who might show up. Our hearts swelled within us as we watched car after car make their way up our gravel driveway, each one carrying someone whose only purpose was to offer encouragement and prayer.

Because of a compromised immune system, Jimmy Ray had been advised against public gatherings. So we opened up the window and he was able to communicate with his church family through the screen. Their words of encouragement and prayers were the boost he needed to persevere until a resolution to his illness would come.

Our Newsong family not only saw to Jimmy Ray's need for encouragement, they also saw to mine. On August 26th, two days after the prayer meeting, CJ's older brother, Jim and his family paid another visit to the barn. This time, they came to celebrate. It was my birthday, and this family wanted to make sure I had something to smile about that day. They brought a homemade birthday cake complete with candles and a lighthearted birthday card to match.

We were unable to celebrate in the upstairs apartment due to Jimmy Ray's advised quarantine. So we celebrated my birthday in the downstairs laundry room. Judy, Jim's wife, lit the candles and they all sang, "Happy birthday, dear Lynn. Happy birthday to you." As unlikely as the venue was, it provided a moment of lighthearted normalcy that had eluded us over the past eight weeks. Little did we realize how much more elusive that sense of normalcy was about to become.

Sometime during that last week of August, Jimmy Ray awakened in the night suffering from another severe headache and asked me to get him something for the pain. By this time, we had a large tin full of medications that had been prescribed by a number of different physicians. I didn't know which pain medication could be taken with certain others and feared giving him something that would create an adverse reaction. I stood paralyzed as I peered down onto a host of prescription drugs, including an assortment of painkillers. I felt helpless and confused. I didn't know which one to choose.

121

Jimmy Ray pleaded with me to call a pharmacist to inquire about interactions, but it was nearly midnight and I had trouble finding a pharmacist working that hour. He snapped at me to hurry, not out of anger, but out of an anguish that yearns for relief. I was finally able to track down a pharmacist who enlightened me on possible interactions, and I gave Jimmy Ray one of the pain killers deemed safe. But I felt remorse for having taken so long to get him the medication he needed, and wished it were not up to me to make these decisions.

I was overwhelmed. Not only had I been put in charge of tending someone I was completely unqualified to care for, but I was now carrying the full responsibility of the church. I had spent the entire month of August performing all of Jimmy Ray's pastoral duties as well as the church bookkeeping and business related to the land purchase. I wanted desperately to help him and to see the church remain intact until he recovered, but I felt inadequate and unqualified for both of the tasks that had just been thrust upon me.

One morning in early September, Jimmy Ray awakened with severe pain in his side – the symptom of an inflamed spleen. Fearing his spleen might have ruptured, I rushed him to the ER at Washington Regional Memorial Hospital in Fayetteville. Thankfully, his spleen was still intact, but the doctors and specialists there were determined to find a resolution to his illness and began to subject him to every blood test and every procedure they could devise that might lead to a course of treatment.

One of the first specialists to see us was Dr. Hennigan, a renowned infectious disease doctor in the area. After ordering and reviewing the results of a number of blood tests, he sat down to talk with us. When he walked into the room, I was wearing a paper gown, mask and gloves required of all those who entered Jimmy Ray's room. "You can take that mask off," Dr. Hennigan said. I looked at him puzzled. Then he looked at Jimmy Ray. "You don't have mono," he said. Now Jimmy Ray and I were both confused. For nearly two months, we had been under the assumption that Jimmy Ray was fighting a severe case of mono that had been merely complicated and compounded by other conditions.

Jimmy Ray did have an enormously high EBV count, which usually indicates mono. But Dr. Hennigan realized there was something else at work here and ordered a liver biopsy that he felt might hold the key. Unfortunately, it would lead to no new answers. I sat in Jimmy Ray's room waiting for him to return from the biopsy. They wheeled him in and returned him to his bed. He was terribly bruised and sore from the procedure that he described to me as "barbaric." But it was over now, and he soon drifted off to sleep.

About 30 minutes later, a nurse came in to check Jimmy Ray's vital signs. She attempted three times to get a blood pressure reading but failed each time. With a look of concern, she left the room and returned with an older, more experienced nurse. After she tried three times, the older nurse called in an emergency team. A group of six or seven doctors and nurses rushed into the room and began to quickly assess Jimmy Ray's condition. His blood pressure had gone so low they were unable to get a reading, and his heart was beating dangerously fast.

Jimmy Ray awakened during the commotion, but said little. He simply watched and responded to their questions when asked. When I saw the urgency in their faces and heard how dangerously abnormal his vitals were, I feared I was watching God's warning of Jimmy Ray's death unfold before my eyes. God had told me Jimmy Ray would die in the fall of the year, and today was September 4th – not quite officially fall, but close enough in my mind. Could Jimmy Ray be dying before my very eyes? Even after eight and a half years of contemplating his death, in that instance I found myself completely unprepared, even shaken.

After several minutes of frantic activity, all the medical personnel left the room and began making arrangements to have Jimmy Ray moved to the ICU. We were left alone in the room, both stunned by what had just happened. He looked at me with concern in his eyes and spoke with uncertainty in his voice. "Lynn, what's happening to me? This is what happens to people when they die."

I walked over to his bed, leaned over his face, and began to gently run my fingers through his hair. "I don't know, Sweetheart, but as long as you have breath, I'm praying life over you." The next day was September

5th, and was our 22nd wedding anniversary. It certainly wasn't the relaxing getaway we had envisioned, but I was just thankful Jimmy Ray was still with me. Only one day earlier, I feared he was dying before my very eyes.

"It's our anniversary," he said softly as I neared his bedside. "I should be kissing you." His eyes watered as he attempted to hold back his tears.

"Don't you worry, Sweetheart. There'll be plenty of time for that when you get well," I responded softly and kissed him on the forehead.

Over the next two weeks he would continue to suffer at the hands of some very determined but very perplexed doctors and specialists. He would also experience the continued deterioration of his condition as the effects of this mysterious illness spread throughout his body.

Part of his left cornea simply sloughed off, and his ophthalmologist had to sew the left eye shut until it healed. One of his lungs filled with fluid and over a liter of what Jimmy Ray described as "dirty pond water" had to be drained and tested. A layer of soft tissue sloughed off the roof of his mouth, and he had to use a numbing mouth rinse in order to eat, lest the condition make it too painful. Eventually painful bedsores formed as he lay in bed day after day.

I remember more than one occasion, when presented with a new challenge he would lie in his bed, close his eyes, shake his head back and forth and declare, "I will not be bitter. I will not be bitter." He did not want to accuse in private the Lord he had so passionately worshipped in public. And although he must have felt at least a part of the desperation Jesus must have experienced when he cried out from the cross, "My God, my God, why have you forsaken me?" he knew his Lord had not left him and he entrusted himself to God's wisdom and care.

After fifteen grueling days of diagnostic tests and experimental treatments, Jimmy Ray was released from the hospital. His attending physician had arranged a host of follow-up appointments with area specialists. The team working on his case was leaning toward an auto-immune disorder, which they thought might respond to steroids. But there was little more they could do for him at this point, and he was eager to get home.

We took Jimmy Ray to his parents' home when he was released from the hospital. They had a downstairs bedroom that meant he wouldn't have to climb the staircase at the barn. Not only that, but he had been so ill for so long and I had become so run down and weary myself, I thought it a good idea to have George and Carol nearby in case I needed their assistance.

The second night at home was particularly difficult for Jimmy Ray. The steroids he was taking made him restless and unable to sleep. Sometime during the night, I was awakened by a thud. The room was dark except for a few rays of light that originated from an outside lamp across the street and streamed through the blinds across the floor. I looked over to see Jimmy Ray in a heap about half way across the room. He was trying to get to the restroom, but collapsed before he could reach the door.

"Sweetheart, what are you doing?" I asked. "You need to wake me up when you need something," I instructed him gently as I helped him off the floor. I threw his arm around my neck and I helped him the rest of the way. After he lay back down, he continued to have trouble sleeping.

He finally drifted off sometime around 7 a.m. After he was asleep, I got up and dressed for the day. When I left the room, I made sure to take with me my purse and anything else I might need for the day. It was my hope Jimmy Ray would sleep for at least a few hours, and I didn't want to awaken him by opening the bedroom door that squeaked when opened or closed.

But about an hour later, I heard a faint voice. "Lynn?" It was muffled at first, so I didn't realize right away it was Jimmy Ray calling my name. Then it came again, this time a little louder. "Lynn!"

I went quickly into the bedroom and around to his side of the bed to see what he needed. "What is it, Sweetheart?" I asked.

Jimmy Ray, with his eyes still closed but his head turned in my direction said, "I think I've sweated through my clothes. I need a clean t-shirt."

I looked down at his t-shirt, not having noticed at first due to its dark brown color, to see that it was soaked with blood. His whole left side from his shoulder to his waist was ringing wet. Blood was oozing from the wound where a port had been inserted at the hospital and then removed before he left to come home.

"George!" I called to his dad with great urgency.

George came quickly into the room, Carol not far behind. "He's bleeding. We need to get him to the clinic!" I said franticly.

We managed to get Jimmy Ray into a fresh shirt, and George applied pressure to the wound while I drove and called ahead to the clinic. It was only a few minutes' drive, and I wanted to make sure they were prepared for us when we arrived.

Nurse Carla, who was all too familiar with Jimmy Ray's case, rushed him into an examining room and immediately began working to get the bleeding stopped. As she applied hard pressure, I noticed her glance with serious concern at another nurse across the room as she shook her head back and forth. She was trying desperately to get the bleeding stopped, but she couldn't get the wound to clot. The clinic called for an ambulance to transport Jimmy Ray back to the hospital.

When word of the day's events spread, here came our kids to take care of us. They were a welcome sight. CJ and his wife Jen arrived in Fayetteville soon after we did. A little later, his older sister Julie arrived with a sack lunch for me in tow. CJ insisted on staying with Jimmy Ray in the ER examining room while I took care of the necessary admission papers and got at least a bite to eat.

Jimmy Ray spent the rest of that day and the next two nights in ICU. His condition continued to deteriorate as more of his internal organs were affected. CJ, like a good soldier, kept a night vigil at the hospital so Jimmy Ray would have someone close by while the family went home to get some rest. Sometime during the night, Jimmy Ray asked a nurse to call CJ into the room.

"Yes, Pastor Jim?" CJ said when he entered. Jimmy Ray was quite weak and it was difficult for him to speak. So he called CJ over where he could whisper in his ear.

"CJ, I want you to get that warrior spirit back." CJ had served in the military for a time before being discharged with an injury, so Jimmy Ray knew his instructions would resonate with CJ's warrior heart. "I want you to stand in front of Newsong and call them to be prayer warriors... not prayer warriors for me, but for Newsong and what God wants to do there." Jimmy Ray's admonition resonated deep within CJ's heart, and when he returned the following Sunday he followed his orders diligently. In Jimmy Ray's absence CJ took a commanding role, leading Newsong in more fervent prayer, in a passionate pursuit of God, and in their continuing mission to reach out to God's lost sheep. When I returned the next morning, Jimmy Ray's bandages were still blood-soaked; the wound in his shoulder had been bleeding for two days. He had a new mask covering his nose and mouth to help him breathe. His weakened voice made it difficult to hear him through the thickness of the mask, but he managed to tell me of the night he had had. His vital signs had gone haywire in the night and once again a team had been rushed in to stabilize his condition. He looked at me as I imagine a child looks at their mother, fearful of something unpleasant or painful. "Lynn, I think they thought I was gonna die last night." I stood speechless by his bedside. I gazed back at him, hoping he could see in my expression the love I had for him even through his blurred eyesight. But I had no words. "I don't want to leave you a widow," he said as his voice broke and his eyes filled with tears.

I couldn't bring myself to respond with any word that would affirm my concern he wouldn't live. But the message God had whispered to me eight and a half years earlier resounded like a carillon in my mind. I feared he would not survive.

"Don't you worry about that, Sweetheart," I responded. "You just worry about getting better."

Later that evening as I sat in the waiting room, I expressed my concern that Jimmy Ray might not live to a friend of the family who was there to offer support. I was taken aback by her response as she began to scold me for my negative confession. She started quoting scripture at me and told me I knew it was not God's will for Jimmy Ray to be sick. I sat there for what seemed an eternity as she lectured me on my need for faith.

But I did have faith. I had faith that what God had revealed he would surely bring to pass. And I had faith that, even if this is not what we wanted or prayed for, if Jimmy Ray died, God would somehow use his death to accomplish an eternal purpose. I believe some in the Church at large have done a disservice to its followers by conditioning them to believe they can have anything they pray for if they only have faith enough to receive it. If they don't receive what they pray for, it's because they simply lack the necessary faith. But your faith has not been truly tested until you've prayed desperately for one outcome, received a different outcome and can still say with complete resolve, "I still have faith in YOU, God."

One need not read further than Hebrews 11 to understand even those set before us, as examples of the very highest faith, did not always receive what they asked for. Verses 39 and 40 of this chapter say, "All of these, *having gained approval through their faith, did not receive what was promised*, because *God had provided something better* for us, so that *apart from us they would be made perfect.*"

As humans, we want answers, we want closure, and we want to know *why*. Believing someone didn't receive what they prayed for simply because they did not have sufficient faith explains away unanswered prayer and wraps up our quandary in a tidy little package. Whether right or wrong, it provides a convenient answer to that nagging question of "why?" But it does not allow room for God to work in ways that are higher than our own or bring about outcomes more concerned with his eternal purpose than with our present comfort.

We must have faith. Without it, it is impossible to please God. But our faith must be in God alone – in his character, his wisdom, his sovereignty and his love - and not in any outcome. We must also take the utmost care not to lay the unnecessary burden of guilt for unanswered prayer on the backs of those already laden with sorrow.

With Jimmy Ray's condition deteriorating and a remedy outside the grasp of his medical team, his attending physician talked to us about sending Jimmy Ray to Mayo Clinic in Rochester, Minnesota. Jimmy Ray's will to live was strong. He had much to live for. So after a very brief deliberation between him and me, the decision was made to transport him to Mayo Clinic the following morning, assuming his attending physician was successful in making the necessary arrangements.

Over the next 24 hours, we were blessed by the outpouring of concern of dozens of our friends, family members and of course, our kids.

A minister friend from Indiana drove over 1200 miles round trip just to pray for Jimmy Ray. On Saturday, a string of Newsong family members, our kids from RFA and many other friends and family came to the hospital to offer their support. He was weak and unable to visit with everyone, but each one who did come to his room that day received a special word of encouragement from Jimmy Ray along with the challenge to "Go after God!" If this was to be his end, he was determined to make the most of it.

CHAPTER TEN

A Puzzle Comes Together

After hours spent coordinating with the Mayo Clinic and medical jet transportation services, Jimmy Ray's attending physician informed us he would be transferred the next morning. "This is the easiest transfer to Mayo Clinic I've ever coordinated," she said. We hoped the ease of his transfer was a sign from God that Jimmy Ray's answer would be found there.

There were so many responsibilities to cover before we left and little time to make arrangements. But in our time of greatest need, our kids stepped in and took charge. Jim Brummett and his wife coordinated with the rest of the Brummett clan to make my hotel arrangements and covered my first week's hotel expenses in Rochester.

CJ began oversight of Sunday church services and coordinated different speakers from within the Newsong family to cover Wednesday nights. Mark, Mary and friends from Pastor Jonathan's church took care of worship on Sundays. Ryan, whom we referred to as one of our "grand-kids," was still a toddler when we left our position at RFA. Now a senior in high school and aspiring musician, he volunteered to lead worship on Wednesday nights. His parents, Virgil and Sue, babysat our truck and the church trailer, making sure set up and tear down at the school happened each week, while Frankie continued oversight of the children's ministry.

Annette, our first girl, took charge of our personal obligations. She made sure our cats were fed and watered and had a fresh litter box. She also took charge of our finances in my absence. I gave her access to my checking account and asked her to make sure our upcoming bills were paid on time. One does not hand over their checkbook on a whim, but Annette was a trustworthy "daughter," put into our lives by God himself. With our church and personal business in the capable and trustworthy hands of our kids, we turned our attention to the matter at hand.

On Sunday morning, September 20th, Jimmy Ray was rolled onto a medical jet; I boarded right behind him. It felt like being enveloped in a tiny cocoon. The plane was terribly small with room for no more than six people, as I recall; the pilot, co-pilot, two medics, one patient and one family member. I remember how surreal it felt taking off the runway as I sat at the head of Jimmy Ray's gurney. This was the kind of experience you hear other people talk about – not the kind you live through.

I was still convinced there was some kind of spiritual connection between Jimmy Ray's illness and Newsong's land purchase, and remained hopeful his answer would come when the deal was complete. Pastor Gary Wheat, who was overseeing the land closing in Jimmy Ray's stead, informed me the closing was set for the following Tuesday, September 22nd. "You're going to get your answer on Tuesday," I proclaimed to Jimmy Ray. "That's when Newsong closes on the land."

When the med-jet landed in Rochester, Jimmy Ray was taken by ambulance to the Intensive Care Unit of St. Mary's Hospital, which is part of the Mayo Clinic system. They wasted no time getting started on his case. He was interviewed extensively and then began a long barrage of diagnostic blood tests and procedures. He groaned as he saw the nurses in charge of drawing blood enter the room. He had already been subjected to dozens of needle sticks and IV's over the past month, and cringed at the thought of starting over. But he was determined to get well and willing to endure whatever discomfort it might entail.

Monday was a brighter day. Pastor Roger Coleman, the young man Jimmy Ray had hired to be his first youth minister at Ellettsville, came for a three-day visit. He and his wife Sharon were pastoring a church in Northern Indiana, and were enjoying successful ministry there. It was an eight-hour drive for Roger, but Jimmy Ray had been a spiritual father and mentor to him, and like a good son, Roger was determined to be by Jimmy Ray's side in his hour of greatest need.Pastor Roger was a Godsend. He not only offered spiritual and moral support to George, Carol and to me, but he was the only person who seemed to be able to make Jimmy Ray laugh; and the laughter was welcome indeed.

Early Tuesday morning, the day Newsong was to close on the land, Jimmy Ray seemed in particularly good spirits. He spent the morning entertaining both Pastor Roger and the medical staff with his favorite movie quotes and show tunes. His favorite quotes came from the most humorous movies he had seen, such as "The Princess Bride" and "Nacho Libre." The return of his smile and usual good humor lifted all our spirits that day.

Sometime late morning, Jimmy Ray's attending physician stopped by for his usual morning consultation. He told us they were working very hard to find the root of this mysterious illness. Jimmy Ray, hopeful his answer would come that day, the day of the land closing, expressed his hopes to the doctor. "Doc, please try hard to give me an answer today. We have reasons for believing today is the day." The doctor smiled and assured us they would do everything in their power to return with an answer soon.

Carol came into the room sometime during the afternoon to check on Jimmy Ray's condition. Pastor Roger and I were already in the room. As I was updating our friends on Facebook and reading Jimmy Ray his latest messages, I read one from a missionary friend in Africa. He said he wanted Jimmy Ray to come overseas and share his testimony of healing as soon as he got well. As soon as I read the message, the mood in the room changed. Jimmy Ray's jovial demeanor turned serious. He closed his eyes, raised his hand toward heaven and began to pray. He motioned for Carol, Pastor Roger and me to come over to his bedside.

As he prayed, the powerful presence of God filled the room as I have never known it before or since. It was a power and a presence that can scarcely be described by words on a page. One must experience it to comprehend it.

As he prayed, he reached his hands out toward Pastor Roger. He put his hands first on Pastor Roger's head and prayed, then on his eyes, then his ears and his mouth. It seemed odd and yet significant at the same time. We weren't quite sure what God was doing in that moment, but we knew something was happening in the spiritual realm - something powerful, something strategic. The four of us in the room knew God had just allowed us to be part of something special, and it left us feeling encouraged.

But the encouragement did not last long. Pastor Gary Wheat called to let me know the land closing had to be postponed until the following Monday, September 28th. We felt so sure Jimmy Ray's answer would come on the day of the land closing, and the fact it had been put off yet again set up a sense of dread. We feared it would now be yet another week before the answer came. What had started out as a hopeful day ended with a visit from Jimmy Ray's attending physician informing us a diagnosis continued to elude them. The week went on with more tests and few answers.

It was sometime that same day that Pastor Roger and I made our way down to the cafeteria to get a bite to eat. My appetite was slight. The last three months of mounting stress had aggravated my gastroparesis making eating a chore for me. But I knew I had to eat to live and to keep up some strength, so I tried to force-feed myself a few bites of something every few hours.

After we went through the cafeteria line Pastor Roger and I found a table next to a window that looked out onto a beautifully landscaped courtyard. The view of God's creation was a calming one. And the artistry of the fall colors was a reminder to me of the majesty of the God who was holding us now.

"You know Lynn," Roger started, "I know God heals. I preach God heals. And I'm praying and believing God will heal Pastor Jim. But as a pastor, I have a hard time knowing what to say to people who pray for their loved ones to be healed and they die anyway."

Roger's dilemma was a familiar one to me. I had wrestled with it when my father was dying with cancer. I knew God still heals. I had witnessed my mother's healing from a number of serious health issues. But how does one reconcile the truth that God heals with the truth that, even as a loving God, he doesn't always choose to?

"You know Roger, God taught me a valuable lesson when I lost my dad. And it's this: The same God who said, 'I am the God who heals you,' also said, 'it is appointed unto man once to die.' The timing of that appointment is up to God."

"You know, I never thought of it like that before," Roger said. "But it makes sense."

After we finished our dinner, Pastor Roger and I made our way back up to Jimmy Ray's room.

Our hearts were saddened when Pastor Roger had to leave us on Wednesday, but he assured us he would be back with Sharon at the end of the week. It was something happy to look forward to in the midst of Jimmy Ray's deteriorating condition and the disappointing news that a diagnosis, and therefore a treatment, was yet to be found.

It was on Thursday evening that a diagnosis was finally confirmed. Jimmy Ray was suffering from hemophagocytic syndrome caused by the Epstein-Barr virus (EBV). His entire body, including his liver, kidneys and even his bone marrow were saturated with EBV. The overwhelming presence of the virus in his body had set up hemophagocytosis, a condition in which the blood begins to consume itself. The immune system becomes confused between what is foreign and what is not and begins to consume the blood cells that control normal clotting functions and fight disease.

Hemophagocytic syndrome is extremely rare and is almost never found in adults. In fact, the doctor charged with Jimmy Ray's care said he had only treated one other adult with the condition, and this, at the Mayo

Clinic, one of the world's most renowned medical facilities, known for diagnosing and treating rare diseases.

"Is there any treatment?" I asked.

"Chemotherapy is the only treatment," the doctor responded. Having watched my dad go through a round of chemotherapy for cancer, I was not anxious for Jimmy Ray to suffer the same fate. But this was the only option we were presented, and if he wanted to try it, I would support him.

Later that evening a representative was sent in to discuss chemotherapy and to answer any questions we might have. Jimmy Ray had only one. "How long do I have if I don't take chemotherapy?"

"Maybe two weeks," she responded matter-of-factly, yet with compassion in her voice.

When she left the room, I asked George and Carol if Jimmy Ray and I could have a few moments alone to discuss our only option. The mood was expectedly somber when they closed the door behind them.

We joined hands and prayed together for God's guidance. When we finished, Jimmy Ray was reminded of a passage from Deuteronomy 30. He quoted from the passage, "'I [God] have set before you life and death…choose life.' I want to live," he said. "I choose life." Jimmy Ray's will to live was strong. So he grabbed hold of the only option he had been given and made the decision to start chemotherapy.

Late the next evening, a nurse came in to prep Jimmy Ray for his first chemotherapy treatment. However, when she took his vital signs, she became quite concerned and called in a couple of doctors to evaluate his condition. They were eventually followed by a larger team of doctors and nurses who began to work frantically to stabilize his vital signs. His blood pressure had once again dropped dangerously low and his heart was beating dangerously fast. They needed to start pumping fluids into his system immediately to bring up his blood pressure.

I sat helplessly by as attempt after attempt was made to get an IV started. His arms were black and blue, as though they had been struck repeatedly with a club. He had been stuck so many times his veins had developed a thick scar tissue, which was preventing the smooth insertion of an IV. Unable to start an IV in either arm, one of the nurses pulled his sock off and started looking for a promising vein in his foot. Up to this point, I had been stoic. I had held up for the sake of the church and for Jimmy Ray. But this was more than I could bear. I bolted from my chair, out the door and headed down what felt like an endless hallway to an empty waiting room. I found a seat in the corner where I sat down and began to weep. Jimmy Ray was dying, and I knew it. But worse than that, he was suffering. I could more easily handle death than I could the suffering that often accompanies the process of dying. Yet here I was again, left helpless to witness this heart-wrenching scene of his life slowly waning, just as I had witnessed my father's.

A young, slim, dark-haired nurse entered the room shortly after I did and sat down next to me. "I thought I would find you here," she said. "He has the best doctors in the world taking care of him. This is exactly where he needs to be. He's going to be okay," she said as she tried to console me.

But I knew better. It was hitting home to me that I truly was witnessing God's revelation of Jimmy Ray's demise come to pass before my eyes. When the nurse realized her words were having little effect, she patted me on the shoulder and returned to her station.

A few minutes later Carol found me and sat down in the chair next to mine. She put her arm around my shoulder and asked, "Are you all right?"

"No! I'm not all right!" I responded. With that declaration my stream of tears became a flood. I sat with my elbows on my knees, my face in my hands, rocking back and forth as I sobbed uncontrollably.

Carol moved from her seat and got down on her knees in front of me. She put her right hand on my left shoulder and her left hand on my right forearm. "You know what? He has the best doctors in the world," she started. "He's gonna take this chemo and he's gonna get better and everything's gonna work out, I just believe it." What a dear woman. Her heart was assuredly in anguish as profoundly as mine, yet her attention was focused on consoling me.

But none of those who tried to comfort me knew what I knew. None of them had been made privy to the warning of Jimmy Ray's death as I had. I knew how this was going to end, and my heart was in anguish.

I had prayed so many times that if God were going to take Jimmy Ray, his passing would be quick and painless. I could not bear to see him suffer. But my prayer had not been answered.

"Why?" one might ask. Why would God not answer a prayer that a loved one be taken quickly, easily, painlessly? Perhaps it is for those of us who are left to see more clearly the contrast between what this life has to offer and the life that is offered to those who die in Christ. It is easier to release someone when you know you are releasing them from a life of suffering into the loving hands of the One who will make them eternally whole.

Friday night, September 25th, without ever having begun chemotherapy, Jimmy Ray was transported by ambulance back to the Intensive Care Unit at Mayo Clinic's St. Mary's Hospital. It was a dark day, but Saturday was made brighter with the return of Pastor Roger, this time with his wife Sharon. Pastor Roger and Sharon brought rays of sunshine and much needed ministry to all of us Severns. They were warm and caring, and they made it okay to feel weak, because you knew they were there to be strong for you.

News of Jimmy Ray's deteriorating condition prompted the arrival of other friends and family members. His brother and sister-in-law, aunt and uncle came from Northwest Arkansas. My brother Billy and his wife Cindy came from Missouri and a dear friend of my mother's drove her up from Southern Indiana. It was a comfort to be surrounded by the loving support of so many family members and friends.

But for all the loving people who surrounded me, there came a moment of panic as I sat in the waiting room. It was that same sense of panic a small child most assuredly feels when they find themselves separated from their parent in an amusement park or shopping mall. Realizing I would soon be left alone without my husband, the one I had loved and leaned on for 22 years, I looked at my sister-in-law Cindy and with a frightened tone asked, "Who's going to take care of me?"

"Don't worry, Lynn. You've got a lot of people who love you and are going to take care of you." But I had never lived life alone. I had lived with my parents until I entered college, lived in a dorm until I graduated, lived with my parents until I was married, and had spent the last 22 years, over half my life with Jimmy Ray. It was an overwhelming, frightening thought to be left alone without him.

But my heart was calmed as I thought about the eight and a half year period of preparation God had allowed me. Surely, if God had loved me enough to prepare me for this eventuality eight and a half years in advance, he had already made provision for my care.

Sunday night actually turned into a night of poignant memories for the Severn family and for Pastor Roger and Sharon as we gathered in Jimmy Ray's room. Jimmy Ray was quite taken with Sharon's robust alto voice, and began making a number of song requests. He was heavily medicated, but still coherent enough to enjoy the people around him, and he was ready for a little music. "What's that song you used to sing at Ellettsville, Sharon?" Jimmy Ray asked.

"Ummm, I'm not sure which one you mean, Pastor Jim. 'His Eye is on the Sparrow', maybe?" Sharon responded.

"Yeah, that's the one! 'His Eye is on the Sparrow.' Sing that one."

Sharon broke into the first verse as Jimmy Ray directed her with his hands. "Why do I feel discouraged? Why should the shadows come?" her voice rang out.

"No, no!" he stopped her all at once. "That's the wrong key. Sing it in a key we can all sing in," he instructed her.

Sharon responded with a hearty chuckle. She was more than happy to comply and started to sing in a number of different keys, but she seemed to have trouble finding one to suit him. Then, all at once, she hit a sweet spot, and we all sang along as best we could.

George and Carol, Pastor Roger and Sharon, and Jimmy Ray and I stayed up until 4 a.m. talking, laughing and singing together. He wanted nothing more than to be surrounded by those he loved most, and we were more than willing to oblige.

Sometime late in the afternoon on Monday, September 28th, I

received a call from Pastor Gary Wheat, our sectional presbyter who had been in charge of Newsong's land closing in Jimmy Ray's stead. He informed me that he and another of the Arkansas District officials had signed the closing papers that afternoon. Newsong Church was now the proud owner of five acres of land directly adjacent to Gamble Elementary School, where we had been meeting over the past year and a half. It was nice to hear some good news for a change.

I got another boost when I received a call from CJ telling me he, his sister Julie and "our first girl," Annette were in the car headed to Mayo Clinic. They had heard how Jimmy Ray's condition was deteriorating and wanted to spend some time with him and with me. They had gotten a late start due to CJ's work schedule and wouldn't be in until around 3:00 the next morning. But they were on their way.

Having been awake until 4 a.m. and spent most of the day at the hospital, I was in dire need of some rest. Not only was I sleep deprived, I was malnourished and had lost a great deal of weight over the past three months. Pastor Roger bought me a small package of peanuts in hopes of getting some protein into me. But only minutes after consuming them, I had to make a quick trip to the restroom to regurgitate.

Sometime early that evening, my brother Billy and his wife Cindy took me back to the hotel to rest. After a short visit and organization of food and luggage it was time to go to bed. The three of us lay down around 10 p.m., but we all had difficulty drifting off to sleep.

Around 10:30, I received a call from Carol. Her message was short and to the point. "Lynn, this is Carol. He just passed."

"We'll be right up," I responded.

On September 28th, 2009 at 10:23 p.m. Jimmy Ray Severn went to be with his Jesus whom he had so passionately loved and worshipped. On the very day Newsong Church had closed on their land, Jimmy Ray had gotten his answer from the Lord. The answer was, "It's time to come home, Son. Your work is done." This young man of 44 years, who had loved and mentored dozens of young men and women and who had taught more than one generation to go after God with all their being, was now gone from this earth, not having accomplished a fraction of what he had in his heart to do. But Newsong's land deal was now complete, and so was his work.

Billy, Cindy and I quickly dressed and headed back to Mayo Clinic. I was mentally, emotionally and physically at the end. But when I walked into Jimmy Ray's room that night, it was not sorrow or panic or even fatigue that overwhelmed me. I was instead overwhelmed by the peace and comfort of an Almighty God. It was that peace that transcends understanding spoken of by Paul in Philippians 4. The weight of the message God had whispered to me eight and a half years earlier suddenly lifted, and God's wisdom in sharing it with me would start to come together like the pieces of a puzzle.

The first ones I called with news of Jimmy Ray's passing were Pastor Roger and then CJ. I thought perhaps CJ, Julie and Annette would turn around and head back home. But CJ was insistent they continue on to Mayo Clinic. As CJ had anticipated, it was after 3:00 a.m. when they drove into the parking lot.

When they arrived they found the doors to the hospital locked, but a security guard allowed them in. They had hoped to find family still lingering, but we had all gone back to our hotels by that time.

"We're all exhausted. I think we should get a hotel room and head back after we've had some sleep," Julie said.

"You and Annette go on ahead without me. I'm going to stay here," CJ said. CJ had been an armor bearer to Jimmy Ray. Militarily speaking, that is one who sees to any and every need of his commanding officer. While many find purpose in leading, CJ had found his purpose in serving his mentor, his leader and his friend. Jimmy Ray had leaned heavily on CJ during Newsong's start-up. Now that his leader had fallen, CJ found it impossible to leave. He felt the duty a soldier feels when his commanding officer falls in the field. And just as he had kept the night vigil when Jimmy Ray was in the hospital in Arkansas, CJ kept the night vigil in the Mayo clinic lobby. It was as near as he could get to his now-fallen leader and friend.

Billy, Cindy and I headed for home early the next morning. As soon as I arrived back in Northwest Arkansas, I began making funeral arrangements. I could think of no better place to have the service than Gamble Elementary School, the place Newsong Church called home. Of course, I could think of no more fitting tribute than to have his "kids" take charge of the service.

I asked Brad, the young minister who had first called Jimmy Ray about starting Newsong, to preach and asked Pastor Roger Coleman to handle the gravesite service. Ken, another one of our kids from RFA agreed to lead worship. CJ saw to logistics and made certain the room had been properly prepared for the service.

Darrell, the young man Jimmy Ray had taught to play the bass guitar two decades earlier, put together a beautiful tribute video. And eight young men and women from Northwest Arkansas and Ellettsville, including one of Jimmy Ray's dear cousins, asked if they could share something about the impact Jimmy Ray had on their lives.

When the day of the service came, you had only to look from the front of the cafeteria to the back to see the impact this man had made. I stood in awe as I watched 300 people make their way into Gamble Elementary School to celebrate Jimmy Ray's life. Over 50 of the attendees had traveled nearly 600 miles from Indiana to be there.

I found myself scanning the room for any of our kids who may have come. And everywhere I looked there was a face that brought back a memory of a happier time. However, in my effort to not overlook any of our kids either present or past, there was a face from the past I did overlook. It was Jimbo. He had found himself there quite by accident.

Desiring to offer his condolences in person, Jimbo hitched a ride from a couple of staff pastors from his church who thought they were going to the viewing. But there was some miscommunication about viewing and service times, and they found themselves at the funeral instead. Seeing how focused I was on visiting with others who were there – others more a part of my present than my past – Jimbo refrained from making his presence known to me at the time. He didn't even sign the guest book. Six months would pass before I was made aware he had made the effort to come.

I could not have felt more loved or honored by those who came to celebrate Jimmy Ray's life that day. It was a day befitting a man who had given his all to go after God and to reach the lost sheep to whom he had been sent.

On Saturday, October 3rd, after a celebration of a life well lived, Pastor Jimmy Ray Severn was laid to rest. Eight and a half years after God first whispered to me I would lose Jimmy Ray as a young man, and that I would lose him in the fall of the year, I stood at his gravesite as Pastor Roger, Jimmy Ray's spiritual son, committed his body to the ground.

I could now see the wisdom in God's eight and a half year preparation. With Jimmy Ray gone, the responsibility of Newsong Church fell to me. No one but God could have known eight and a half years earlier that I would be called upon to shepherd a baby church through the sickness and death of their pastor. And no one but God could have known that I personally would be offered the task of finding the pastor who would succeed Jimmy Ray. But God knew. In his wisdom he had given me the time necessary to process Jimmy Ray's death, so I would have the emotional strength and presence of mind necessary to keep the church going through the transition. He had also given me a clue as to who should follow Jimmy Ray at Newsong. It had to be a spiritual son; this much I knew.

The church in Ellettsville organized a memorial service for those in Indiana who were unable to attend the funeral in Arkansas. I was invited to speak and gladly accepted the invitation.

I arrived at my mother's home in Indiana a couple days before the memorial service. While there I began to pray hard about which spiritual son of Jimmy Ray's I should contact about taking his place. I had already contacted one about the possibility of pastoring Newsong, but he was on a path to foreign missions and felt God wanted him to remain on that track. As I prayed more fervently, I felt impressed that I should contact Pastor Roger and Sharon Coleman. I had decided not to call them earlier, as I knew they were aware the church was open and assumed they would contact me if they were interested. But while I was waiting on them to call me, they were waiting on me to call them.

Little did I know Pastor Roger and Sharon had been talking with each other and praying about the possibility of coming to Newsong. They knew it would be a monumental task, as following either a planting pastor or a pastor who has died always is. They would be facing a double challenge. But their hearts were drawn to the church, and they were willing to go if God would but make it clear this was his path. So Sharon set out a fleece before God. "Oh God, if you want Roger and me to go to Newsong, please have Lynn call us."

I reluctantly made the call to Pastor Roger and Sharon, as I had assumed they were uninterested. I remember the tone of Pastor Roger's voice when I asked him, "Have you given any thought to coming to Newsong?"

There was a bit of nervous laughter and a hesitation to respond. I continued, "I'm going to be in Ellettsville for Jimmy Ray's memorial service. If you're interested, I'd like to meet with you to discuss it."

As God would have it, Pastor Roger and Sharon had already made plans to make the four-hour trip from Granger to Ellettsville for the memorial service. Feeling certain my phone call was an answer to Sharon's fleece, the Colemans agreed to meet to discuss the possibility of becoming Newsong's next pastors.

I remember our meeting at the Olive Garden Restaurant. Sharon seemed convinced they were to come, but I sensed a hesitancy in Pastor Roger. As I shared with them and solicited their thoughts as well, it became apparent to me what Pastor Roger's hesitation was. He simply felt inadequate to fill the shoes of his spiritual father and mentor. His personality and skill set differed from Jimmy Ray's, and he was concerned he might not be up to the challenge.

But I was feeling more and more confident that Pastor Roger was the spiritual son God had ordained to follow Jimmy Ray. I became even more confident as Pastor Roger reminded me of the powerful prayer time he, Carol, Jimmy Ray and I had experienced on that Tuesday before he died. Pastor Roger recalled how Jimmy Ray had laid his hands on his head, his eyes, his ears and his mouth, as though he were blessing or commissioning him. I realized as he shared, just what had taken place in that hospital room that day. God was transferring his anointing, his power and blessing for ministry, from Jimmy Ray to Pastor Roger that day.

Newsong Advisory Team, taken the day Newsong became a self-governing church, Front: Pastor CJ, Lynn, Pastor Roger, Virgil Back: Cappy, Don

As Pastor Roger sat looking unsure of himself, I looked him straight in the eye, quite sure of myself and said, "Roger, if God thought Newsong Church needed Jimmy Ray Severn, Jimmy Ray Severn would still be here." My assertion seemed to strike a chord. I continued, "You have a different personality and a different set of skills, but you are who Newsong Church needs."

As the evening wore on, the three of us, Pastor Roger, Sharon and I became more convinced they were to follow Jimmy Ray at Newsong. I invited them to come and minister the last week of October so they could get a better sense of their mission field and solidify what we believed God was whispering to each of us.

Pastor Roger, Sharon and their two daughters spent that last weekend of October in Northwest Arkansas. They had the opportunity to get acquainted with our Newsong family at an all-church picnic on Saturday and Pastor Roger preached on Sunday. The church was abuzz, and hopes that Pastor Roger would be our next shepherd began to surface.

Feeling confident we were hearing God clearly, I extended an invitation to Pastor Roger to follow Jimmy Ray as Newsong's shepherd. All that was left was the approval of the church planting committee who had been responsible for Newsong's inception. The meeting with the committee was relaxed and brief. It seemed their consensus was that if I approved of the Colemans, they approved of the Colemans. After all, who better to trust with a baby than its mother? The committee looked to me as Newsong's mother and felt they could trust my decisions for her care. Without hesitation the committee put their stamp of approval on the Colemans.

Pastor Roger and Sharon loaded up a moving truck and made the move from northern Indiana to Northwest Arkansas. Our Newsong family wanted to ensure they felt at home the minute they pulled into the drive. So they decorated their house with Christmas lights and had a meal already prepared when they arrived.

On December 20th, 2009, Pastor Roger and Sharon began their new mission at Newsong Church. I was overwhelmed as I looked back over the past eight and a half years. Little by little I had watched as the revelations God had whispered to me unfolded. As I pondered recent events, my mind was taken back even further to the eight week revival we had been part of when we first moved to Ellettsville as youth ministers. I recalled the message God had whispered to me through one of his dear servants during a time when I so doubted my effectiveness and purpose in ministry. She had said, "God has something for you to do that nobody else can do." I had wondered what might be the special role only I could play, and now that role had been both revealed and completed.

As Jimmy Ray's wife, I had been called by God to lead our baby church through the sickness and death of her shepherd. And as directed by God, I had appointed a spiritual son to follow him. God had allowed me the advance preparation and the grace I needed to complete both of those missions. The puzzle pieces that had so long perplexed and distressed me had finally come together to create a nearly complete picture. Only one piece remained.

Before Jimmy Ray and I ever left Ellettsville to move back to

Arkansas, God had whispered to me that my life would reflect that of Ruth in the Bible. And as I could now see, my life was truly forming that reflection. Like Ruth, I too had been widowed at a young age. Like Ruth, God had plucked me from my own home and family and planted me in the land where my husband had been born and raised. Like Ruth, I had been called to bless my mother-in-law after the death of her son. And like Ruth, I was enjoying the benefit of a home and land provided through the benevolence of my late husband's family. But there was yet one part of the reflection that remained hidden. Who, if anyone, would be my Boaz?

CHAPTER ELEVEN

FINDING BOAZ

There's something about being alone in the middle of God's creation that makes you slow down and ponder things. I remember standing alone at the barn, looking out my big picture window across the adjacent pasture and the woods beyond. I was pondering how the next chapter of my life might read. "Oh God, no one is ever going to cherish me the way Jimmy Ray did," I said under my breath. Our marriage had been tried by fire just a few short years earlier, but God had brought us forth as gold. A bond had been forged between us that only death itself could have broken. I couldn't imagine life with anyone else making me smile the way life with Jimmy Ray had.

The pondering was short-lived by necessity, though. Those first three months before Pastor Roger and Sharon arrived provided little time to mourn and even less time to map out a possible future. There were too many duties that required my immediate attention. My life was consumed with caring for the church and handling all the personal business that follows the death of a spouse.

Thankfully, God had provided a host of earthly angels to lighten my load. These were the same ones I had come to know on a path of ministry I had tried so desperately to avoid when I was young. Our kids from RFA, our Newsong family and our Ellettsville church family all joined together to support me during this pivotal time.

Frankie, one of our girls from RFA who was overseeing our children's ministry, organized a group of women called "Lynn's Ladies." It was their mission to meet any need I could conceive. Whether I needed someone to run errands, buy groceries, do yard work, or just needed a shoulder to cry on in the middle of the night, they were at my beck and call 24/7. It gave me a great sense of security knowing they were there and willing if ever I needed them.

The ladies from Newsong organized meals for me, which was a most welcome treat. It not only released me from the burden of cooking, but the families who brought meals stayed to eat with me. Their company during such a lonely time was as much a blessing as their home-cooked meals.

CJ, along with Felicia, another one of our girls from RFA, endeavored to see that Jimmy Ray's medical bills were covered. They rallied dozens of our RFA kids and Newsong family members and sponsored a medical benefit concert. They not only raised enough to cover all of Jimmy Ray's medical expenses, but there was enough left over to present two scholarships to our alma mater in Jimmy Ray's name. Jimmy Ray would have been so very proud could he have seen the way his kids stepped in to assist me in his absence.

Jimmy Ray's dad, along with the men of Newsong took on various other tasks to see that my home and yard were cared for. They bush-hogged, repaired lawn equipment, made heating and air repairs and installed insulation in the barn. Daniel, our sound man, who was also quite computer savvy, set up a new computer for me and helped me with the technical aspects of closing Jimmy Ray's graphic design business. It seemed my sister-in-law Cindy had been right. I *did* have a lot of people who loved me and were willing to take care of me. And as I sit, putting pen to paper, I am once again struck by the fact I met each and every one of these on a path I had tried so desperately to avoid – the path of pastoral ministry.

George was especially helpful to me those first few weeks after Jimmy Ray's passing. It seemed every few days, if not every few hours, I was calling on him to help me attend to tasks or make decisions I had never been responsible for making on my own. It was George who taught me how to drive the lawn tractor, make simple home repairs and made sure I got the best deal on my first car purchase. But there was one of these occasions that turned into a special moment I shall never forget and will always cherish.

It seems in our haste to move into the barn Jimmy Ray had failed to arrange our final building inspection. A few weeks after the funeral, I got a call from someone at the county inspector's office asking me if the barn had ever been completed.

"Yes, we finished in the spring and I've been living here since April 1st," I answered.

"Oh, really?" she said. "You should have had a final inspection and gotten an occupancy permit before moving in."

"I had no idea," I responded. "My husband was taking care of all that and he recently passed away."

I felt myself getting flushed - apprehensive about any repercussions that might stem from our moving in before our final inspection.

"I'm so sorry for your loss," said the lady from the inspector's office. "Can I arrange for someone to come out and do your final inspection? The sooner we can get this taken care of, the better," she said. It eased my mind somewhat to hear both concern and sympathy in her voice.

Unsure of who would be sent to my house or what code violations an inspector might find, I called George to see if he would come up for the inspection. He and Jimmy Ray had built the barn practically from the ground up, and I knew he would be more qualified to address any construction issues than me. He was more than willing.

A few minutes before the inspector was to come, I heard George's pickup coming up the gravel drive. When I saw his truck crest the hill, I went downstairs to open the garage door for him.

He stepped out of his pickup and walked slowly toward me. He approached me with a look of care and concern. Then he put a strong, fatherly arm around my shoulder and hugged me close. The smell of freshly cut hay was still on his overalls. "How are ya doin', Hon?"

"I'm doin' okay, George."

"Well, you're doin' better than I am," he said as he rested his cheek on the top of my head. His eyes turned red with tears and I felt his sorrow as I heard a muffled sob.

"We're gonna be okay, George," I said with assurance. "We're gonna be okay."

"Are we?" he asked.

"Yes, George, we are," I responded with certainty.

In that moment my mind went back to the Mayo Clinic, just minutes after Jimmy Ray had passed. My mom, having lost my father eight years earlier, realized how much support I would require as I adjusted to life on my own. She looked at George and told him, "Lynn's gonna need you more than ever now, since she doesn't have her own daddy anymore."

It seemed Mom had been right. In my own father's absence, it was George I had turned to and leaned on during those first few weeks after Jimmy Ray passed. He had provided the practical help that I needed, and my assurance that we would survive this tragedy seemed to give him the hope that he needed. And out of our mutual need, a bond was created between us –a bond that surpasses that of in-law to in-law. George became my father that day, and I became his daughter.

The inspector drove up only minutes later. He offered his condolences to me as soon as he stepped from his truck. Thankfully he found only three minor issues that were quickly and easily taken care of by George and me. I breathed a sigh of relief as he handed me my occupancy permit and drove away.

I was humbled but not especially surprised by how George and my entire Newsong family were taking care of me. They had often demonstrated compassion and support of others whom life had rendered needy or broken. However, there came an offer of assistance that did surprise me. Only days after Jimmy Ray passed, I received an e-mail from Jimbo. His brother Randy, a pastor in Indiana, had received word of Jimmy Ray's passing and alerted Jimbo to the news. Jimbo was quick to offer his condolences and assistance at Newsong:

"Lynn, my brother just sent me news about Jimmy Ray. I'm so sorry to hear about this.

Know that I join the many others who are praying that you will know God's own comfort at this time.

If you need any short-notice supply preaching at the church - or other help- let me know.

Grace and peace, Jimbo"

After our brief and rather impersonal encounter at JBU, I had not expected any communiqué from Jimbo. It was not that he had been rude or off-putting during that meeting. It was just that the encounter had seemed to me completely emotionless. It was not that I expected to give or receive even a platonic display of affection, given the fact I was married. But our encounter had seemed to lack the slightest expression of warmth or even the casual smile that often accompanies the surprise meeting of two old friends after many years apart. The encounter had felt to me more like a business meeting than a reunion.

I responded to his e-mail with a brief "Thank you for your offer..." and a short paragraph sharing that God had been preparing me for this eventuality, although I did not go into detail. I did not take him up on his offer of assistance at the time, however. There were a couple reasons for my reluctance. My first concern was, of course, for the church. I had never heard Jimbo preach and was uncertain about how he might be received by our congregation. He had not only earned a law degree, but had also earned a master's degree in theology and a Ph.D. in religious studies, and I was concerned his material might be over all of our heads. To be quite frank, I was afraid he would bore our people with a lecture that was too abstruse. I wasn't willing to invite him without doing my homework first.

My second reason for not asking for his assistance right away was a more personal one. He had hurt me...*deeply*. And although I had moved on to find my destiny and many years of happiness with Jimmy Ray, there was a past that would have to be dealt with. At the time Jimbo e-mailed me with his offer of assistance, I had yet to make it through Jimmy Ray's funeral. I simply did not have the emotional energy to take even the first step down that path. Perhaps that day would come, but today was not that day.

The first two Sunday services following Jimmy Ray's funeral were preached by another dear friend, Rev. Cecil Culbreth. Cecil had been the Arkansas District Youth Director when Jimmy Ray and I were youth ministers at RFA. Cecil had taken a liking to Jimmy Ray and had been a profound influence on his life and ministry.

Cecil and his wife Patti were eager to take me under their wing. Having both lost spouses themselves, they understood the pain and uncertainty that come with widowhood. Even though they realized they could not remove the pain itself, they wanted me to know they were at my side to walk the journey with me.

Patti seemed particularly eager to offer her support. We soon became Facebook friends and kept in touch via e-mail. I had felt an immediate bond with Patti and felt as though I could share any thought or emotion with her. There was nothing I could share with her that she didn't understand. Although she has since gone to be with Jesus, her compassion, insight and wisdom, which I will share a bit later in the story, would prove invaluable to me. I will always be thankful to have called her my friend.

By the time November rolled around, I had successfully scheduled most of the Sunday morning services through the end of the year. I had scheduled a number of repeat speakers to maintain some sense of continuity from week to week. We had, however, pretty well exhausted our resources when it came to Wednesday nights. A number of our Newsong family members had willingly taken one or two services, for which I was most grateful. But each week was handled by a different speaker, and I felt our congregation would benefit from more continuity. Having had a few weeks to recuperate both physically and emotionally, I decided it was time to contact Jimbo for assistance. But first, I needed to make one important call. I needed a reference from his pastor, Gary Wheat, who had seen to Newsong's land closing in Jimmy Ray's stead.

"Hey Pastor Gary, this is Lynn Severn."

"Well, hello Lynn! How are you? What can I do for you?"

"I was wondering if Jim Blankenship goes to your church," I said.

"Why yes, yes he does," Pastor Gary replied.

"Have you ever heard him speak?" I asked.

"Why yes, yes I have. As a matter of fact I've had him preach for me several times. He teaches an adult Sunday school class for us too."

"Well…" I said and then hesitated a brief moment, "is he any good?" I asked, with a bit of a snicker.

Pastor Gary laughed. "Yes, he's done a very good job every time I've heard him. I haven't been to his Sunday school class myself, but I hear good reports from there too."

"Does he talk over everybody's head?" I asked, as I continued to press for information.

"Well, he *is* very knowledgeable and that comes through in his preaching, but he's able to bring his message down to a level that seems relevant to everyone."

Pastor Gary's recommendation was good enough for me. With the assurance Jimbo would be able to present a meaningful and relevant message to our Newsong family, I shot an e-mail off to him asking for his help. I needed five Wednesday night services covered during November and December, and Jimbo eagerly accepted the invitation to cover all five.

It was a tremendous burden off my shoulders to have all of Newsong's services scheduled through the end of the year. By this time, I was confident Pastor Roger and Sharon would be in place by Christmas, and I looked forward to turning the reins over to someone else. Getting the rest of the year's services scheduled was just one more responsibility I could mark off my list before the Colemans arrived.

Is It God Or Am I Crazy?

The introduction of Jimbo back into my life introduced a whole new set of uncharted and at times awkward situations for me. Our history made it impossible for me not to at least consider the possibility of our reuniting. But it was so soon after Jimmy Ray's passing. If we did start spending time together, how would my friends, my family, and most of all George and Carol perceive it?

Before Jimbo came to fill in that first Wednesday night at Newsong, I felt compelled to talk to Carol about how she and George might feel if and when I started dating again. It wasn't that I felt I needed their permission, but I desired their blessing. They had become a second set of parents to me, and the last thing I wanted was to jeopardize that relationship or to cause them greater pain.

I was reluctant to broach the subject at first. But if Jimbo and I did start spending time together, I didn't want them to be taken unaware. It was an awkward and difficult conversation to start, but I knew it was a necessary one.

I stopped in at Carol's one afternoon as I often did. Like so many times before, she offered me a cup of coffee and we sat down at the kitchen island for a chat. My heart began to pound as I mustered up the nerve to bring up Jimbo.

"Carol, I've got something to ask you."

"What is it, Hon?" she asked.

I hesitated just a moment and took a deep breath. "How do you think you and George will feel if and when I start dating again?"

Much to my surprise and without a moment's hesitation she responded, "Go for it." I was stunned by how quickly she came back with an answer – and a positive one at that.

Of course, this was just like George and Carol. They were the kind of people who would say and do the right thing regardless of how it affected them personally. Carol continued, "George was saying to me just the other day, 'Lynn's still a young woman. She'll probably get married again. And if she does, that's okay. She fulfilled her vows to Jimmy.'"

While I felt relieved by George and Carol's blessing, I knew it would be harder for them to accept if and when a new relationship became a reality for me. I knew seeing me with another man, whether Jimbo or someone else, would only be a painful reminder that their own son wasn't there.

"Well the reason I'm asking is because I've asked Jim Blankenship, the prof from JBU that I dated in high school, to come and fill in for us at Newsong. I don't know how he might feel about me, and I don't know how I feel about him. But considering our history, I think there's a possibility of dating again."

Carol's eyes drooped just a little. It was one thing to verbalize her blessing when the prospect of my dating was hypothetical. It was quite something else to really consider what my being with someone else might mean for them. How would it feel to see me on the arm of another man? Would he accept them? If I remarried, would I sell the land they had passed to Jimmy Ray? Would I marry again and disappear from their lives altogether? I'm sure all of these questions were going through Carol's mind when I told her about Jimbo. But she was resolved to encourage what she thought was best for me.

"If that opportunity comes your way, you go for it," she repeated. "You fulfilled your vows to Jimmy and there's no sense in you spending the rest of your life alone."

I was once again struck by the strength and character of this woman. Her response was completely selfless. The Severns' love and support of me made me more determined than ever to remain a part of their lives. I had felt God's call to be a blessing to Carol before we ever left Ellettsville, and her love for me made it the easiest and most joyous task God ever asked of me.

I left Carol's house that day feeling some sense of relief. I realized, though, that whoever my Boaz was, whatever he was like, however long it was before I found the one God had for me, my relationship with another man would be a long and challenging adjustment for the Severns. If and when that time came, I was determined to do all I could to make that adjustment as easy as possible. I knew they didn't want to lose me to someone else, and I certainly didn't want to lose them.

It's curious isn't it, how, regardless of the passage of years, there are certain situations that leave us feeling like children again. That was quite assuredly my experience the first Wednesday night Jimbo came to speak at Newsong.

Although I wasn't entirely optimistic, I knew there was a chance Jimbo and I might be reunited. After all, looking solely at the circumstances that had brought us both to this part of the country at this time in our lives, it could easily be assumed the arrangement was nothing short of divine. Yet God had taught me we cannot always discern his path based on circumstances alone. What often may appear to be his path on the surface, may actually lead to disappointment.

The anticipation of seeing Jimbo for the first time in over 26 years as a single woman conjured up a myriad of questions as well as a few butterflies. The last time I had seen him under these circumstances was when he had kissed me good-bye for the last time and drove away, never to return. But that was 26 years ago. Who was he now? How would I feel about him? How would he feel about me? Had the possibility of our reuniting crossed his mind, or was he too settled into bachelorhood to even consider the possibility?

I arrived at the church office where we held mid-week services about an hour ahead of time to start. I wanted to make sure the restroom was clean, the meeting room was vacuumed, and the coffee was brewing before others arrived.

I had bought a new outfit for the evening, due partially to the fact I had lost a significant amount of weight, weighing just barely over 100 pounds, and owned little that still fit. And for the sake of complete honesty, I'll admit I was also motivated by a desire to create a charming look for Jimbo. I picked my outfit carefully. I wore a new pair of grey-blue jeans, a silky apple green blouse and an ivory sweater that tied above the waist. I finished the ensemble with a matching necklace and earrings. They were made of hand-blown glass and the pendant hung from a short, thick, shiny green cord. I deemed it to be the perfect ensemble to achieve that "I-want-to-look-cute-but-not-too-eager" effect.

As time for the service drew nearer, I began mingling with a few of the early-comers. I was calm and relaxed on the outside, but my stomach was churning on the inside. I felt like I was 16 again, waiting anxiously for that special someone to arrive. I hadn't been this nervous since before Jimbo took me out on our first date. My mind was teeming with questions. What would we talk about should he arrive early? Would he perceive that I was nervous? Since our parting in 1983, he had gone on to earn three graduate degrees. Would he find my attempt at conversation trite or foolish?

6:40 rolled around – twenty minutes before service. I stood against the back wall peering across the room through the front glass door. The image of a tall, middle-aged, silver-haired man wearing a pair of dark-rimmed glasses at the tip of his nose blocked the sun and cast a shadow across the floor. The door swung open quickly and Jimbo stepped inside.

"Good evening," I said with a smile.

"Good evening," he responded in his deep, bass voice as he walked toward my side of the room.

"How was the drive over? Did you have any trouble finding the office?" I inquired.

"No. No problems at all. I drove right to it."

His appearance was quite different from the Jimbo I had known more than a quarter of a century earlier. Had it not been for our brief encounter at JBU, I would not have recognized him. But every once in awhile he would form a word a particular way or make a certain familiar expression, and I would catch a glimpse of the Jimbo I had known so long ago.

As soon as 7:00 rolled around, I asked the group to take their seats and opened the service. After I gave the week's announcements and led in a few worship songs, it was time to introduce Jimbo.

"I'm very pleased to introduce our speaker tonight, Dr. Jim Blankenship from John Brown University," I began. I took the next few moments to bring the audience up-to-speed on Jimbo's education and accomplishments. After the obligatory listing of his credentials, I felt obliged to let the audience in on a bit of our history.

"Dr. Blankenship and I actually attended the same youth group together in Indiana back in the early 1980's," I said, relaying nothing of our past dating relationship. I caught Jimbo's eye. "Can you believe that's been over a quarter of a century ago?" He looked a bit surprised as it dawned on him just how long it had been and even made reference to the time that had passed when he took the podium.

I took my seat on the second row at the far right side of the room. I listened intently as Jimbo eloquently explained insights into God's Word none of us had seen before. Pastor Gary had been right. Jimbo was quite knowledgeable and it did come out in his teaching. But he had been able to turn years of in-depth research into an attainable and applicable lesson. I was both pleased and proud of him.

I spent the evening observing Jimbo, trying to gain a sense of just how time had changed him. I was pleasantly surprised at how open he was with our people and how easily laughter came for him. He had seemed much more serious and focused on accomplishment than he had on enjoying life when we were dating. I had rarely seen this more relaxed side of him. I found his humor and his ease with others attractive. Perhaps there *would* be a future for us together. But there was so much more we needed to learn about each other.

Jimbo's help at Newsong provided opportunity for chit-chat but little else. There were so many things I was eager to learn about his last 26 years, and questions I still had about our parting that I wanted laid to rest. If only there was an opportunity to sit down face-to-face and catch up on the last quarter century.

But how could I make that happen? I had been raised from the viewpoint that it is inappropriate for a woman to initiate a social engagement with a man. Yet I felt Jimbo would be hesitant to invite me for coffee or to dinner due to the fact I had so recently lost Jimmy Ray. In fact, I felt quite sure he would wait six months or even a year, the time many deem appropriate to grieve a loss, before he would initiate any type of social engagement outside church – that is, if he desired to spend time with me at all.

I shared my dilemma with my new friend, Patti Culbreth. I relayed to her the relationship that had existed between Jimbo and me so many years ago and the unlikely circumstances that had found us both single, in our 40's, and living less than 15 miles apart. She responded with nothing but support and some very insightful wisdom.

"There is nothing wrong with you asking Jimbo for coffee," she wrote. "You are friends, you are both single, and he is ministering at your church at your request." She was right. Guest speakers are often invited for coffee or to dinner by their host ministers. The fact Jimbo and I had a past connection seemed to make it all the more appropriate. It made sense to me.

But her counsel didn't end there. She helped me understand another vital aspect of our rather anomalous situation. "Jimbo will probably be especially cautious because of your recent loss," she wrote. "He doesn't know where you are in your grieving process or when you might feel ready to pursue a new relationship. It will be up to you to guide him – to let him know where you are in that process."

She was right again. There was no way Jimbo could know all the ways God had prepared me for Jimmy Ray's loss. And I suppose, given the way our relationship had ended, he might consider me reluctant to pursue even a friendship with him. After all, he is the one who had done the leaving.

"What have I got to lose?" I thought to myself. I was curious. I wanted to know who Jimbo was today, and there was only one way to find out. So I e-mailed Jimbo to see if he'd be interested in catching up over a cup of coffee. He seemed delighted. Not only did he agree to meet me for coffee, he took it a step further and offered to take me out for dinner at the restaurant of my choosing. He would pick me up at the barn the following Tuesday.

My stomach was in knots as I awaited his arrival on that Tuesday evening. I nervously walked back and forth between the front picture window and the sofa and back to the picture window again. I began to wonder how on earth someone like me was going to converse with someone like Jimbo, a former lawyer, a professor, and a Ph.D. I found myself completely intimidated before he ever pulled into the drive.

But then it dawned on me. Or perhaps it would be more accurate to say God opened my eyes to see. Jimbo had plenty of co-workers and plenty other scholars with whom he could discuss "brainy stuff", as I like to call it. He was surrounded by professionals and professors with whom he could discuss legal, theological or philosophical quandaries. What he didn't have, or so I supposed, was someone to just be interested in him – someone who was interested in his hobbies, his dreams, his disappointments, all the things that made up the man as opposed to the scholar. He needed someone he could relax with, laugh with, and someone who would take his mind off the demands of work and career. What he needed was someone to simply enjoy life with. These were the things on which I would focus.

Just as the clock struck 5:00, I peered out the picture window one more time to see Jimbo's little red car turn past the tree atop the hill of my driveway and pull in front of the garage. I went downstairs to greet him.

He was reservedly cordial but seemed pleased to be there. I invited him in to see the barn. When he got upstairs to the apartment, I asked if he'd like a tour.

"Sure," he said.

"Okay," I said as I directed him to the middle of the room. "Come stand over here, turn around in a circle, and you've had the full tour," I instructed with a grin. It was true, though. Except for the restroom and closet, my apartment consisted of just one room, and the entire space could be viewed completely from anywhere you stood.

I took him over by the picture window and boasted of the view. "Isn't it beautiful?" I asked.

"Mm-hmm," he agreed. "It sure is."

I pointed to a spot in the pasture just to the east of the barn where some cows were grazing. "It's my dream to build a house right there someday," I said. He agreed it would be a beautiful spot for a home.

After his short tour, we left for Mimi's Restaurant in Rogers about 25 miles from the barn. I was actually looking forward to the longer drive, as it would give us plenty of time to visit. Jimbo was intentionally courteous to me. And he was much more talkative than I had remembered him being in the past, giving no evidence that he was nervous in the least. But I wasn't entirely comfortable. As the evening wore on, it became evermore apparent to me that this was not a man I had known for 26 years. This was a man I knew 26 years ago, and there was an obvious difference.

I had not been privy to the details of his life in more than two decades, nor had he been privy to mine. I was unaware of his everyday routines, his interests, his hobbies, and the way in which his extraordinary life experiences had impacted who he was today. He had become, in many respects, a stranger to me, but a stranger I was eager to know once again.

There was plenty of conversation on Jimbo's end, as I quizzed him on just about every aspect of his life I could think of. But I hadn't much to share. My life held little fascination in comparison to his. While I pressed for details about his past 26 years, he showed little interest in mine. In fact, I finally just asked him, "So is there anything about me you would like to know?" I thought surely he would be curious about my college years or life in ministry or the new work Jimmy Ray and I had started in Centerton. But his list of questions for me was a short one. "I really only have three questions for you," he started. "How are you doing? How is your health? And do you have a support system here?"

His questions were obviously evidence of a genuine concern for me. He had taken note that I was quite thin and was concerned for my health. The stress of Jimmy Ray's illness, death and the weight of the church had rendered my frame a shadow of what it had been just a few months earlier. But I assured him my health was improving now that I was getting more rest and nutrition. I also shared with him the tremendous support system God had put in place for me here through Jimmy Ray's family, our new church and our kids from RFA. He seemed pleased and relieved to hear I was being looked after.

The evening was pleasant and confusing at the same time. I enjoyed our time together enough to want to see him again. But I was unsure about whether Jimbo was really my Boaz. I wasn't ready to close the door on this possibility, but I was open to other doors that may be open as well.

November moved along quickly and soon it was time to travel home to Indiana for Thanksgiving. I cancelled the Wednesday evening service prior to Thanksgiving and made sure everything was in place for the next Sunday's service before I left. With all the bases covered, I felt in no rush to return to the barn. A few days to relax at home in Indiana with friends and family was a very welcome change of pace for me.

Home was about a ten-hour drive from where I lived in Northwest Arkansas. And many hours on the road alone meant many hours to ponder what (or who) God might have in store for me. My mind went back to Ricky, the gentleman I had been so smitten with when Jimmy Ray and I were struggling in our marriage. I wondered if he knew about Jimmy Ray's passing, if he had ever married, or if he might ever be interested in me. I wondered if God had perhaps allowed us to get acquainted through my job at IU because he had a future planned for us together.

I made arrangements to have lunch with my very dear friend Betty. She had been for me what Samwise Gamgee had been to Frodo in "Lord of the Rings." For so many years, knowing she could not carry my *burden*, she was faithful to carry *me* with her friendship and her prayers. God had sent her to be my faithful friend through what I often refer to as "my crisis" - those years that felt like being choked by barbed wire. She had also been a wealth of information when it came to Ricky.

"So, Betty, do you know anything about Ricky these days?" I asked over lunch.

"I rarely see or talk to him anymore," she said. "I hear he has a girlfriend, though, and from what I hear he's pretty smitten with her. It wouldn't surprise me in the least if they got hitched."

The news created just a twinge of disappointment, but I had no desire to compete for anyone's affection. I realized this was simply God's way of closing a door he didn't want me to enter. When the time was right, he would guide me as he always had. I just hoped and prayed he would not leave me alone. I had loved being married and loved having someone to share my life with. Being widowed had left me feeling as though half of me was simply missing. Living out my days alone was a dreadful thought. But the thought of living them out with the wrong person was more dreadful by far.

My brother and sister-in-law were unable to make it back to Indiana for Thanksgiving, so Mom and I ate Thanksgiving lunch at one of the few restaurants open that day. After we returned home, we spent the rest of the afternoon sleeping off our turkey and mashed potatoes. Mom's nap lasted a bit longer than mine, so having awakened with no one to converse with I decided to check who might be on Facebook. I got out my computer, logged on, and turned on "chat." Whom did I find online and ready to chat but Jimbo? The conversation went something like this:

Lynn: "Happy Thanksgiving"

Jimbo: "Happy Thanksgiving"

Lynn: "Where are you?"

Jimbo: "I'm at the office. Don't have internet at home."

Lynn: "What did you do for Thanksgiving dinner?"

Jimbo: "I made ham and yams at home."

"Oooh, that's impressive," I thought to myself. I conjured up a mental picture of Jimbo in an apron and baker's mitt, placing his uncooked ham and sweet potato casserole in the oven. A scholar and a cook to boot!

The chat continued.

Lynn: "Really?! That's impressive."

Jimbo: "Not really. I stuck a few slices of canned ham and canned yams in the microwave and called it Thanksgiving dinner."

I quickly went from impressed to sympathetic. I couldn't imagine a more depressing way to spend Thanksgiving Day – alone away from family eating ham out of a can. But it didn't seem to bother him. It seems he had spent many a Thanksgiving Day alone away from family, and what seemed catastrophic to me was customary to this contented bachelor.

We chatted back and forth a bit longer until Jimbo became frustrated with his inferior typing skills. It was decided we should continue our conversation in person after I returned. The conversation did not end, however, until the subject of our past had been touched upon. We agreed both our past, as well as what may be in our future, were subjects that needed to be addressed. But while chatting online can be useful if you're interested only in communicating facts, nothing can take the place of face-to-face communication when you need to communicate motive and emotion. So we agreed to table the details until we could talk face to face.

After I returned from Thanksgiving break, Jimbo and I began spending more time together. Besides seeing each other at church on Wednesday evenings, we tried getting together for dinner at least once or twice through the week. I often cooked for him either at the barn or at his home since he rarely enjoyed the pleasure of a home-cooked meal.

On one occasion, I asked Jimbo over to the barn for an Indian meal. He suggested toting the ingredients over to his house instead so we could cook together. Cooking together sounded much more desirable than cooking alone to me, so I seized the opportunity.

While we were making food preparations, the doorbell rang. Jimbo left me in the kitchen to continue chopping and dicing while he went to the door. It was Diane, the administrative secretary from the Bible department.

"You left these papers at the office," I heard her say. "I knew you were going to need them, so I thought I'd just drop them off on my way home."

"Oh no!" I thought to myself. "It's someone from the school."

Jimbo had expressed to me his desire to keep our relationship under wraps, especially from those he worked with. "If people find out I've been spending time with someone, they'll think I'm on the market. I don't want anyone trying to set me up on blind dates again," he explained.

Aware of Jimbo's wishes to keep our time together quiet for the time being, I retreated to the part of the kitchen most secluded from the living area. I worried Diane would get suspicious that Jimbo had a female guest when she got a whiff of gourmet Indian food.

But much to my surprise, Jimbo seemed eager to introduce me. "Come on out here, Lynn," he said. "I want you to meet Diane."

I was surprised but pleased that he was willing to make my presence known. Little did I know Jimbo had schemed to leave the "forgotten" paperwork at the school so Diane would have an excuse to stop by. She and her husband Dave had been Jimbo's dearest friends since he had moved to the area, and their impression of me was important to him. The scheme to deliver "forgotten" paperwork would give Diane a chance to look me over.

There was another evening spent together somewhere around the same time. I remember it well. Jimbo had come to the barn for dinner. After the meal, we retired to the living room for a cup of coffee and a chat.

166

I sat down on the loveseat and Jimbo took his seat on the sofa. We talked for hours, catching up on the past two decades plus. Nothing was off the table. We discussed not only our journeys, but also how those journeys had changed us. Some events had left us with a sense of accomplishment and pride; others had led to disappointment. We talked about the changes time and experience had wrought, as well as those parts of our character that had remained unchanged. At one point during the evening I observed, "I think we're the same people we were 26 years ago. We're just better versions of ourselves."

But after hours of conversation, there was still one subject that had not been broached by either of us. It was the proverbial "elephant in the room" we had both been avoiding. Were there any old feelings, buried long years past that might be raised to the surface? Did the possibility of a future together exist or not? I was certain Jimbo would avoid the issue for months to come due to the fact I had been so recently widowed. But I wanted an answer. I wanted to know if there was hope of a future together or if I should cut the relationship off now while my heart was still safe.

As inappropriate as it may seem to some and as uncomfortable as it was for me, I took a deep breath and dived in head first. "I know I shouldn't ask this, but…" I paused and looked down at the floor, feeling too awkward to make eye contact. Then I took another deep breath and nervously continued. "Any old feelings?" I inquired.

Jimbo heisted for just a moment, as he formed a careful response. "I'm almost 50 years old," he started. "I've been single a l-o-o-o-n-g time, and very happy being so. The chances of me ever marrying are pretty slim." he said.

"I didn't ask you if you wanted to marry me," I responded. "I just asked if there were any old feelings."

"I know," he said, "but I'm too old to date just for the sake of dating. If I'm not relatively sure I'm going to marry, I don't even want to start down that road."

"Well, that's an honest answer," I said, "and that's all I wanted." I wasn't quite sure how to interpret his answer, though. He hadn't denied having feelings for me, nor had he taken marriage off the table. But he hadn't given me much reason to hope either.

Even though he had kept his deepest emotions veiled, I understood his motive for offering such an ambiguous answer. Even if he felt no romantic affection for me, I knew he cared about me and wanted to protect me. He knew I had just suffered a tragic loss, and he had no desire to add to it. He knew he had hurt me in the past, and wanted to avoid a path that might cause that pain to be relived. He was simply being cautious, and he was doing so for my sake more than he was his own.

Jimbo's caution didn't keep him from spending time with me though. Once a week soon became twice a week, and twice a week quickly became three. And the more time we spent together, the more at ease we both became. The intimidation I had felt our first evening out began to fade as I realized just how down-to-earth Jimbo was. He was indeed brilliant, but he was comfortable living out an ordinary life at home.

One evening after we had eaten dinner at Jimbo's house, he went to put a movie in the DVD player. He noticed there was a disc already in the machine. "Hmm, I wonder what that is?" he asked himself as he took the old disc out of the player. "Oh, it's The Muppets," he said with half a chuckle.

"The Muppets?" I thought to myself as I grinned with amusement. Whatever intimidation I may still have felt was quickly dispelled in that moment. If this man was down-to-earth enough to enjoy the zany humor portrayed by a cast of silly puppets, he was down-to-earth enough for me. I was discovering Jimbo had a highly developed, albeit dry sense of humor, and was actually quite fun to be around. Time with Jimbo was providing something the last few months had left me lacking – laughter. I was finding this new Jimbo even more attractive than the one I had said good-bye to so many years ago, and I quickly found myself falling in love with this man all over again.

December passed quickly and soon it was time to travel home to Indiana for Christmas. With Pastor Roger and Sharon now in place at Newsong, I decided a two-week visit to Mom's was in order. I met my brother and sister-in-law in Springfield, Missouri on the way home and caravanned with them the rest of the way so I wouldn't have to make the long journey alone.

Those two weeks at home for Christmas provided my first opportunity to be completely free from the responsibility of Newsong since Jimmy Ray had passed. I took the opportunity to surround myself with family and my dearest friends who made me laugh the most. I found out during a visit with my dear friend Ruthie, however, that you have to be cautious about just how much laughter you allow yourself to enjoy.

I had found a picture of Jimbo on Facebook I thought was particularly attractive. Ruthie and I enlarged it on her computer monitor, and she took a picture of it while I pretended to kiss Jimbo on the lips. The result was quite convincing and rendered a "kissing" picture that had us laughing so hard I actually strained a rib muscle. I will have to confess, though, there's no better way to suffer an injury than through laughter.

Christmas vacation provided yet another bright spot for me. Jimbo and I began to correspond daily via e-mail. The subject matter was mostly trivial – what activities we had planned with family that day or what friends we might be meeting for dinner. But I also took the opportunity to share deeper thoughts and feelings. I wanted him to know who I was and how I thought, not just what I had accomplished, as he contemplated whether or not to pursue a romantic relationship. I was pleasantly surprised to find he looked forward to my daily communiqués as much as I did his. The daily interaction put a smile on both of our faces.

As we continued to learn who the other had become over the years, I of course asked God if this man was my Boaz. But for some reason, God's answer seemed a vague one to me. There was only one verse he kept leading me back to. "The Lord says, 'I will guide you along the best pathway for your life. I will advise you and watch over you.'" Psalm 32:8 (NLT). Rather than giving me a clear yea or nay as to whether Jimbo was my Boaz, God was asking me to sit back and trust him to provide the counsel I needed as I needed it and to watch his plan for me simply unfold.

Up to this point, Jimbo had been very careful not to categorize our relationship as "dating." He thought our present stations in life, his many years of bachelorhood and my recent widowhood, called for a more cautious approach. His caution had kept him from even the slightest display of affection. I had not received even an arm around the shoulder or a pat on the back, let alone an embrace or a kiss.

But there was an ease I felt with Jimbo that, by this time, had left me with a suspicion we would someday marry. With that suspicion, my friend Ruthie and I went on a diamond safari. I believe we hit every jewelry store in Bloomington looking for the perfect engagement ring before we stopped at a little shop just off the town square. There in the front case was the most beautiful engagement ring and wedding band set Ruthie and I had seen. It was modest but beautifully designed with a marquise diamond in the middle and several small stones in a band that wrapped around the finger like a ribbon. I figured if Jimbo ever did decide he wanted to marry me, I would save him the trouble of having to pick out an engagement ring on his own. I was sure he'd be happy to be saved the legwork, and I would be assured of getting exactly what I wanted.

Since my brother and sister-in-law would be heading back west before me, I e-mailed Jimbo to see if I could follow him back to Arkansas on his way back from Indiana. He was visiting his family who lived in the northern part of the state and would be headed back home at the end of his Christmas break. I wasn't used to traveling alone and was uneasy about traveling such long distances without a companion. I made sure to warn him, however, that traveling with a woman meant extra restroom breaks, and having me tag along would probably add to his travel time. He didn't seem to mind the inconvenience, though, and happily agreed to caravan.

We rendezvoused in Terra Haute, which was about an hour from where I lived, and started on what should be another nine or so hours on the road. And just as I had warned him, less than an hour into our trip I found myself in need of a restroom break. I called Jimbo on his cell phone and asked him to stop at the nearest restroom; it need not be pristine.

He did as I had asked and pulled off at the nearest gas station. It was an unsavory-looking one, but my sense of urgency was such, I didn't mind. We pulled into a gravel parking lot at the side of the station where the restrooms were to be entered from the outside. We stepped out of our vehicles at the same time. There was a rather questionable-looking fellow standing outside between the two restrooms, smoking a cigarette.

Jimbo, uncertain of the man's character or intentions, wanted the man to know I was not there alone. As a protective gesture he put his arm around my shoulder and walked me up to the ladies' room door. He stood outside and made conversation with the smoking man until I emerged. Then once again, he put his arm around me and walked me safely to my truck.

As we traveled on the weather began to change. The sky quickly went from sunny to gray and it began to snow. The precipitation quickly changed from snow to sleet, and soon the windshield of my truck was covered with an icy film.

A nearly constant stream of windshield wiper fluid was all that was keeping the glass clear enough to see. Unfortunately, each time I pressed the button, less wiper fluid came out onto the glass. Before long it quit working altogether.

I called Jimbo to let him know I needed to stop at a gas station to put more wiper fluid in the truck. He found the nearest gas station and we cautiously pulled off the highway onto an exit ramp that was covered with about a foot of thick, snowy slush.

When I exited my truck, I realized I didn't even know how to open the hood. Not only that, but I was so short and the truck was so tall, I couldn't have raised the hood or reached the wiper fluid container if I had wanted to. Jimbo, just over 6 feet tall, easily managed to open the hood and check the fluids. Much to our surprise the wiper fluid wasn't empty; it was frozen. There was no way to unfreeze it, so Jimbo scraped my windshield and used a new bottle of wiper fluid and paper towels to get off the last bit of icy film.

"Let me know when it gets too hard for you to see. We'll pull off and I'll clean your windshield again," he said. Then we journeyed on.

The snow and ice came down in a relentless shower and the roads worsened the further we drove. About every twenty or thirty minutes, we had to pull off and let Jimbo clean my windshield again. Jimbo had no problems with his wiper fluid, but the warm air from his heater against the frigid glass of his windshield caused it to crack from one end to the other. It was a trying day. And what should have been a 9-hour trip turned into a 12-hour one. Thankfully, after a long grueling day and hundreds of miles on treacherous, winter roads, we made it safely back to Arkansas.

Rather than taking his normal exit home, Jimbo was thoughtful enough to see me all the way to the barn. It added another thirty minutes to his trip, but he wanted to make sure I made it home safely and to help me with my luggage once we arrived.

I was so thankful he had been on the journey with me. Had we not been together, I would have been forced to stop at a hotel for the night – not something I was eager to do as a woman traveling alone.

After he saw me home and carried in my luggage, I made myself available for a good-bye hug. "A hug good-bye?" I asked, as he reached for the door on his way out. I thought it was in order considering his arm around my shoulder when we encountered the smoking man. Unfortunately, I had mistaken his protective gesture for a romantic one. He hesitated and remained silent for a moment as he formed a response.

"I really don't want to start down that road," he said, "not until we've made the decision to move our relationship forward."

I was, of course, confused by his reluctance. Had he not put his arm around me twice already that day? I assumed he would want to hug me good-bye, even if he didn't offer a kiss. But he refrained.

I began to wonder if pursuing a relationship with Jimbo was really in my best interest. I was falling in love with him, all right, but I was too emotionally drained from the loss of Jimmy Ray to play guessing games. If Jimbo didn't want to pursue a romantic relationship, I could live with that. I had lost him once before and survived quite well; I could do it again. If he wanted to pursue a more serious relationship, I was happy to embark on that journey as well. What I didn't want was to relive age 16 all over again, not knowing where I stood or how he felt about me. I was simply too drained to juggle that kind of uncertainty and emotional stress.

I had invited Jimbo over to the barn for dinner the following evening, and he came over around 5:00 as planned. I made a pot of chili, which is always a comforting meal on a cold winter day. I made sure to leave the garage door up so he could pull his car right in when he arrived. As soon as he arrived, I heard his car pull inside, the garage door close, and the clomp, clomp, clomp of his footsteps as he climbed the stairs.

Knock, knock, knock, came a rap on the door. I opened it up and let Jimbo inside. "Hey there! How was your day?" I inquired.

"It was good," he said, as I took his coat and hung it on the coat rack.

"Would you like to eat now, or would you like to sit down and relax for awhile first?"

He looked at me and hesitated, but said nothing. I thought perhaps he hadn't understood me, so I repeated the question. "Would you like to eat now or would you like to sit down and relax for awhile first?"

Without saying a word, he took my arm, pulled me toward him and embraced me as tightly as he could without impeding my ability to breathe. He said nothing; he just held me. I kept expecting him to release me, but he seemed averse to letting me go. His long embrace felt as comforting as a warm blanket and a seat in front of the fire after being left outside too long on a cold, blustery day.

His gesture, while welcome, took me completely by surprise. He had been so reluctant to engage in the slightest display of affection the night before. But it felt wonderful to be held. There is little in this world that makes a woman feel as safe or as loved as the embrace of the man she loves. And after the emotional demands that had been placed upon me over the past few months, there was nothing I relished more.

Whatever questions I had about Jimbo's affection for me faded in that moment, as God brought the picture of my Boaz clearly into focus. After more than 26 years apart, we were once again a couple.

Jimbo still needed some time to process the prospect of marriage, but I did the best I could to alleviate any trepidation.

"I'm a good catch, you know," I started, as I made a humorous attempt to convince him he should marry me. "I have no children, no debts, I haven't gotten fat and I haven't gone bald." Jimbo grinned as he listened intently to my argument. "I deserve a good man," I continued. "You should marry me before I find one."

At that he tilted his head back and began to laugh out loud. Although I'm sure the case I had just made for our getting married had little to do with it, our conversations quickly went from, "if we get married..." to "when we get married..." And we began to paint a picture of what a future together might look like.

We kept under wraps for just a few weeks the fact we were now a couple. But sometime in mid-February, we felt comfortable letting others in on our newfound happiness. While there were many who welcomed our news, there were others who questioned, even resented my involvement with someone so soon after Jimmy Ray's passing. But I had lived with death hovering over me like a dark cloud for close to a decade now, and I was eager to embrace life, to embrace joy, to embrace a future for which I was not fixated on the end. I was eager to smile again.

As soon as we made our relationship public, Pastor Roger and Sharon invited us to their home for dinner. I was eager to introduce Jimbo, and they were eager to meet the man who had so quickly won my heart.

While I consider Pastor Roger and Sharon my "kids," they had become quite protective of me since those dark days at the Mayo Clinic. Pastor Roger wanted to make sure anyone I was spending time with was worthy of me and met with his and Sharon's approval. It was to that end that he e-mailed me a humorous list of questions they would have for Jimbo that evening:

1. So Jimbo...what exactly are your intentions with our Lynn?

2. If in the unlikely event that you and our Lynn get serious and she would even consider marrying you... are you going to be man enough to seek my approval for her hand in marriage?

3. Exactly how do you plan to support our Lynn?

4. And in the event that you should hurt our Lynn, you do know Jimbo that I have no problem going back to prison?

When Jimbo was presented with the Roger's list of questions he not only laughed loudly at the humor, but he was struck by the love and concern behind them. It was obvious that, behind the humor, Pastor Roger and Sharon wanted only God's best for me.

Sharon fixed a beautiful meal with ham, potatoes, a lovely garden salad and homemade rolls. The evening was relaxed and conversation came easily. Pastor Roger and Sharon quickly took to Jimbo and he seemed at ease with them. I was happy to see those closest to me accept our new relationship so readily.

A day or two later I was talking with Sharon about the evening. I was eager to get her and Roger's impression of Jimbo and to get a sense of how they felt about my being in a relationship with someone new. "Lynn, I love seeing you so happy. When you were at our house with Jimbo, you were glowing from the inside out. And I loved it!"

Just hearing those words made me both relax and smile. If the Colemans, who were so very close to Jimmy Ray, could be happy for me, then perhaps others would share in my happiness as well.

While the introduction of Jimbo to the Colemans was relaxed, it was time to introduce him to George and Carol. It was a meeting I knew needed to happen, but not one I looked forward to. I knew it would be strange and awkward for all involved. However, if the Severns and I were going to remain a family, we had to get past that first awkward meeting. I didn't want to force Jimbo on them, though, so I left the time and place of that meeting up to them.

Sometime in early March I got a call from Carol. "Hi, Lynn. This is Carol. George and I were wondering if you and Jimbo would want to come over to the house for cake and coffee on Saturday."

"Sure, we can make it," I said. I was happy they were willing to meet Jimbo but I dreaded the meeting.

Saturday rolled around and it was time for Jimbo and me to make our way to the Severns. "Thanks for doing this," I told Jimbo. "I know this has to be hard for you."

"It can't be nearly as hard for me as it is for them," Jimbo responded. "After all, I'll be sitting where their son should be."

We arrived at George and Carol's and made our way to the front door. As usual, George opened the front door before I could even ring the bell.

"Come in," George said as he held out his hand to shake Jimbo's. "Come in and make yourself at home. I'm George."

Jimbo shook George's hand and introduced himself. "Hello, I'm Jim. It's nice to meet you."

Carol made her way from the kitchen. "Hi, I'm Carol. Come on in and make yourself comfortable."

The Severns did their best to make everyone at ease, but we were all uncomfortable for one reason or another. George and Carol's hearts had to be breaking. Seeing me with Jimbo was just another reminder that Jimmy Ray was gone. My heart was breaking for them, and at the same time I felt for Jimbo who was well aware that he was sitting in what used to be their son's seat. And Jimbo was wondering how or even if George and Carol would ever accept him. But despite the awkwardness of the occasion, it seemed everyone was making their best effort to put each other at ease.

Carol and I served carrot cake and coffee while George and Jimbo got acquainted. Once Carol had a chance to sit down, she did her best to engage Jimbo in conversation. She was quite interested in his work at the University and his knowledge of the Bible and church history in particular. Her questions kept the conversation going and kept at bay any moments of awkward silence.

After a thirty-minute or so visit, Jimbo and I excused ourselves and went about our day. It was a relief to have that first meeting behind us. Hopefully, it would only get easier and less awkward from here on.

"They seem like great people," Jimbo remarked as we pulled out of the Severns' driveway.

"Yes they are," I responded. "They sure are."

Within a week or two of that first awkward meeting with George and Carol, a man approached me from Newsong whom God had often used to share special insight or words of wisdom. His name was Art. Art pulled me aside after service, saying he felt God wanted him to share something with me. I had been witness to Art's God-given insights in the past, and was eager to hear what special word God may desire to share with me.

"Lynn, I feel like God wants me to tell you this relationship you're in with Jimbo is from him [God]." I knew this message from the Lord had made an impact on Art, and he felt it was important to share it with me. Art confessed he had been one of those skeptical when Jimbo and I started dating. He had even expressed to the Lord one day in prayer his skepticism about our relationship. But God came back with a terse response in the form of a question for Art. "Well, who are you to decide what's best for her?"

Art and I both chuckled as he relayed the experience to me. I must admit I was chuckling inside for another reason, though. I didn't feel the need for reassurance, and wondered if God's word to Art about my new relationship was more for him than it was for me. But I appreciated his honesty and tucked his words away in my heart nonetheless.

Sometime in late March or early April Jimbo and I made a trip to Indiana to see his nephew perform in a school play. It would be my first introduction to many of his family members and a reacquainting with those I had not seen in many years.

This was the first lengthy road trip we had made together in the same vehicle, and we were curious about how we were going to manage being cooped up in the same small space for nearly 11 hours. But we found the trip a pleasant one.

We arrived safely at Jimbo's parents' home and enjoyed several days with many of his friends and family. It had been a good trip, all in all. But about the third night in, I felt overwhelmed by uncertainty and fear. Just before bedtime, Jimbo had come to my room to give me a hug and a goodnight kiss. He soon retreated to his own room for the night. As soon as he walked out the door and closed it behind him, I had a sudden sense of panic. "What am I doing?" I questioned myself. "I don't even know this man."

At that moment I was overcome by the impact of Jimmy Ray's death and began to wonder how prudent it was to be so deeply involved with someone, even Jimbo, this soon after his passing. My mind and heart were troubled as I lay my head on the pillow that night. So I began to pray.

"Oh, God," I started, "What am I doing? Am I doing the right thing? I need you to tell me for sure if this relationship with Jimbo is right. It scares me and I don't even know why."

Then God whispered to me, as he had always been faithful to do when I needed his guidance. "What did Art tell you?" his voice whispered.

I had been so confident about my relationship with Jimbo at the time Art first relayed his message from God to me, that I had all but put it out of my mind. "He said our relationship was from you, God," I answered, and in my mind I could see God give me a reassuring smile. That was all I needed to ease my mind. God had given me that message during a time I felt so certain, knowing there would come a time I would need to be reassured. I was at peace now, and I would never again question the preordination of our relationship.

Jimbo and I made a trip to the jewelry store on our way back to Arkansas. He wasn't ready to propose yet, feeling the need to get through the stress of the semester before focusing on wedding plans. But he now possessed the set of rings I had picked out the previous December, and we ordered a wedding band he deemed suitable for himself as well.

Sometime in mid-May, Jimbo took me to the AQ Chicken House in Springdale, Arkansas for an early dinner. When we were sufficiently full of fried chicken and mashed potatoes, he nonchalantly pulled out the enchanting engagement ring and dangled it on the end of his pinky. My eyes grew large and an enormous smile formed across my face as I realized Jimbo was ready to make our engagement official.

"Do you know why I chose this restaurant?" he asked.

"No, I don't."

"I *had* to take you out for fried chicken." Then it dawned on me. Jimbo and I had very few pictures of when we dated back in the early '80's. But we did have one treasured set of photos taken at Brown County State Park where we had doubled-dated with Jimbo's friend, Kent and his girlfriend. Kentucky Fried chicken was on the menu that day, and we had more than one picture of Jimbo and me sitting at the picnic table eating our chicken dinners. That day had become a treasured memory for us both.

"Will you marry me?" he asked.

"Yeah, Baby!" I responded with excitement.

I didn't even give him time to slip the ring onto my finger. I immediately took it off his pinky and slipped it onto my ring finger myself. It was not an elaborate, champagne and roses set-up, but to me it was perfect. Jimbo had taken a treasured memory from our past and connected it with an even more momentous occasion looking to our future. I could not think of a more sentimental, more romantic proposal.

CHAPTER TWELVE

HAPPILY EVER AFTER

I spent the next two months putting together what I would consider a simple but elegant wedding. We chose to exchange our vows in a beautiful banquet hall on the Indiana University campus. Where better to celebrate our marriage than the place we had first laid eyes on each other?

On July 5th, 2010, Dr. James R. Blankenship, AKA Jimbo, or Dr. B, as his students like to call him, and I pledged our love and lives to each other. The wedding was held at the Indiana Memorial Union, a sprawling 500 thousand square foot limestone structure with a tower in the middle. More than one stone bridge crosses over a dry creek bed that runs along the structure. It is Indiana's own castle rising out of the midst of endless cornfields.

The dining hall where the ceremony was held is equally majestic. The Tudor room, named for its architectural style, boasts 20-foot ceilings from which hang antique tapestries and red walls donning elegant oil paintings. The front of the room is flooded with light streaming through its limestone-framed, floor-to-ceiling windows. The tables were decorated simply with black and white linens and a single red rose in the center. The venue would have made any bride feel like a princess. It certainly made this bride feel like one.

I wore a champagne-colored, tea-length dress. The skirt was full, but the top was fitted with a ruffle that started at the waist and went around the neck and tucked behind the ruffle on the other side. The dress was complimented with a simple bridal bouquet of white roses and wisps of evergreen. Jimbo was dressed more casual than most grooms, choosing black trousers and vest over the traditional tux.

Guests were greeted by both Jimbo and me and invited to enjoy a cup of punch and classical music as they waited for the ceremony to begin. We enjoyed this more relaxed, less traditional approach as it gave us

DonyaFaith Phtography ©2010
The wedding party left to right:
Kent, Betty, Lynn, Jimbo, Sharon, Monty, Ruthie

time to enjoy the company of those who had made the effort to share this special day with us.

When the last pre-service song began to play, the wedding party casually took their places at the front. Then Jimbo's brother, Rev. Randy Blankenship opened the service. He prayed, greeted the guests and thanked them for coming. But what does one share at the wedding of two people in their 40's? What words of marital wisdom does one impart to a pastor's wife and a Bible scholar?

"Now what can I say today to these two," Randy started, "to my brother, the biblical scholar and Lynn who spent many years in pastoral ministry?"

He went on to reiterate the fact that Jimbo and I already knew about covenants, about God's plan for marriage, and that marriage is a picture of Jesus and his bride, the Church. But despite the challenge, Randy seemed to find the perfect words for the occasion.

"Lynn, for the last ten to fifteen years my brother has been blind. Now I'm not talking about macular degeneration or a detached retina." There was a slight pause and then he went on to explain. "My brother has been blind to women." The crowd chuckled as Randy explained how he and others would often draw Jimbo's attention to an attractive woman only to be amazed and disappointed by his disinterest.

"For a number of years he has been a proud, unabashed, self-proclaimed boycotter of relationships and more than content in his professorial bachelorhood." There was another slight pause before he continued, "But in his blindness...he saw you." Randy then looked at me as his voice broke ever so slightly. "Lynn...you made my brother see." I was moved by Randy's words. I felt my throat tighten and a tear well up behind my eyes. But I would not be shedding tears today. This was a day to laugh.

"And Lynn, my wife recently posted a picture of you and some others in the family on Facebook. Underneath it she wrote, 'Look how adoringly Lynn looks at Jimbo.'" I smiled as I recalled the picture and the comment I wrote underneath. Randy said, "You Lynn, commented, 'Well who wouldn't?'" Everyone was smiling out loud at this point. It was evident

183

Jimbo and Lynn enjoying a fried chicken dinner, 1983

Lynn and Jimbo enjoying another fried chicken
dinner at the wedding, 26 years later

DonyaFaith Photography © 2010

Jimbo and I saw something different, something special in each other as Randy would go on to explain.

"You see, you two have both had your eyes opened...You've seen something in each other that no one else sees...You've seen the will of God."

How true were his words! God's hand in our marriage was undeniable. When we recalled our separate journeys and the unlikely events that had brought us back together, we could do nothing but stand in awe of his divine plan. God's promise that he would have a Boaz waiting for me was being fulfilled in that very moment.

Jimbo repeated his vows to me and then it was my turn. My vows to Jimbo included a portion from the book of Ruth as I recognized Jimbo was my Boaz, given to me by God after a tragic loss. "Where you go I will go, and where you stay, I will stay. Your people will be my people and your God my God." Ruth 1:16b (NIV).

God had truly done for me what he had done for Ruth. He had taken me back to my late husband's home, he had bound me to his family, he had provided me land through that family, he had taken my husband to heaven, and in the midst of my grief he had brought me joy again through my own Boaz.

When the ceremony concluded, our guests were treated to a fried chicken dinner. We chose fried chicken as our main course because it took Jimbo and me back to that fried chicken dinner we had shared at Brown County Park nearly three decades earlier. In lieu of a traditional wedding cake, we chose a chocolate fountain with a myriad of dipping treats. I knew it was a hit when I spied hints of chocolate on the mouths and clothing of numerous guests leaving the banquet hall after dinner.

It was a beautiful day, perfect in every way. A journey of grief was ending and a journey of joy had begun.

I wondered how Jimbo would take to married life after having been single for nearly five decades. But he seemed to take to his new role quickly. On the way back to Northwest Arkansas from our honeymoon in Tennessee, we made a stop at Wal-Mart to gas up the car and stock up on a few supplies. Once inside, Jimbo asked if I would help him find a particular item. I can't recall just what it was now. After we both looked up and down several aisles, I finally spotted what he had been looking for. I saw him walking the other direction so I called to get his attention.

"Jimbo," I called. No answer.

"Jimbo," I called a little louder. Still no answer.

"Jimbo!" I called louder still, and still no response.

He obviously wasn't hearing me, so I tried another approach.

"Husband!" I called. Immediately Jimbo turned around and answered, "What, Shug?" He was taking quickly to his new title.

After we arrived back home in Siloam Springs, I made a trip over to the barn to check on Noah. I had lost Kitty to a serious thyroid condition just two months earlier. George and Carol had stopped in every day or two to make sure Noah had everything he needed while I was away. And on the days he came to the door, Carol was sure to give him a pat on the head and extra treats. Unfortunately, I would not be able to take Noah to Jimbo's home in Siloam Springs when we returned. Jimbo was allergic to cats and more than a day or two in the same space became a misery for him. So Noah would have to reside at the barn alone. He had always been somewhat of a loner, though, and didn't seem to mind having the barn to himself.

When I arrived at the barn after the honeymoon, I was met not only with a very happy cat, but also with a very special wedding card lying on the table. It was from George and Carol. I knew my marriage to Jimbo had brought them both comfort and pain. On the one hand, they wanted to see me happy and to know I was being looked after. On the other hand, Jimbo's presence in my life only accentuated the absence of Jimmy Ray in theirs. And I'm sure they wondered if they would lose me too, now that I was part of another family. Would I remain in their lives or would I slowly drift away? They may have been uncertain about my intentions toward them, but they wanted me to know for sure how they felt about me.

I opened the card and read their words inside:

"Just a note to let you know how much love and happiness we wish for you in your marriage and your new life… Please always know that we will ALWAYS LOVE YOU as a daughter, just as we do now… We pray that we will always remain close. All our love always,
George and Carol."

Words cannot describe the gratitude I felt for their blessing on my new life. Although seeing me with Jimbo was a reminder of their pain, they embraced him and welcomed him as part of the family. They opened their home and their hearts to him as they had me nearly 24 years earlier. And just like their note had promised, they continued to treat me as their own daughter.

Sometime in September George met me up at the barn while I was there seeing to Noah. When I saw his truck pull up in the drive, I went down to visit with him. "Hey, I've got you a Christmas present at the house," George said.

"A Christmas present?" I responded. "It's only September."

"Yeah, I know it, but I've got one for you so you need to come up to the house and get it."

I laughed with surprise and delight. I couldn't imagine what it could be, but I figured if he had tracked me down at the barn to let me know about it, it must be something he really wanted me to have and pronto.

"Okay, I'll be over to pick it up just as soon as I finish taking care of Noah," I said.

After taking care of my chores at the barn, I made the six-mile drive over to George and Carol's. George was waiting on me when I got there. As soon as I walked in the door here he came with a long, narrow cardboard box. It wasn't wrapped, but I still couldn't tell from the packaging what was inside.

I laid the box down on the table and opened it up. Inside was a small, .410 shotgun. "You bought me a shotgun?" I asked with a quizzical smile. I had never owned a gun, but George had learned that Jimbo and I both shared an interest in target shooting. He must also have remembered how much fun I had shooting coffee cans off the fence the first time I came to their house back in 1986. George grinned with pride when he saw how much I liked and appreciated his gift. I couldn't wait to come back with Jimbo and do some target shooting on the farm.

Not too many weeks later, in mid October, we had the perfect opportunity. My dear friend Ruthie came for a weekend visit. It seemed she enjoyed a little target shooting herself. So she, Jimbo and I headed for the Severn farm for one of Carol's famous home-cooked country spreads and to put a few rounds into some old Folgers cans.

It was a memorable evening. Both George and Jimbo helped me get my gun loaded and gave me helpful pointers. Each of us took our turn shooting and then retired to the house for dinner. Somehow that night seemed to be a turning point for Jimbo, the Severns and myself. The awkwardness that had been there at the beginning seemed to be fading and the presence of Jimbo in my life was becoming less painful for George and Carol. They wanted us to be a family, and they were making every effort to make that possible.

As that first year wore on, Jimbo and I easily settled into our new life as a couple. I had feared Jimbo would have difficulty sharing his life and space with another person after spending so many years alone. But surprisingly, he seemed to adjust quickly and easily. That first year together was filled with much laughter and treasured times together as a new couple.

I spent close to a year turning what had been his bachelor pad into a home we could both be comfortable in. But we both longed for a home in the country. Jimbo had grown up in the country and missed the solitude and serenity it offered when he left home back in 1979. God had fulfilled many of the promises he had made to me before I left Ellettsville, but there was one promise that had not yet been fulfilled. He had promised me a permanent home on the land he had given me.

There were three verses in particular God had directed me to when he made that promise. The first two were given to me as God prepared me for Jimmy Ray's passing and were found in Psalm 37. Verse 3 says,

"Trust in the Lord and do good. Then you will *live* safely in the land and prosper." And verse 29 says, "The godly will possess the land and will *live* there forever." These were not only promises of land, but promises of *living in* the land God would provide.

The third verse was given to me as I wrestled with giving up my home in Ellettsville for the sake of starting Newsong. It is found in Matthew 19:29. "And everyone who has *given up houses* or brothers or sisters or father or mother or children or property, for my sake, will receive a hundred times as much in return..." In my heart, I knew God was whispering his promise to me of a home on the property Jimmy Ray and I had received from George and Carol. The only question was when.

"Perhaps when I retire," Jimbo said in the beginning. We were living only a mile from JBU where he taught and the convenience of a two-minute commute was hard to deny. If we built next to the barn the commute would take closer to 30 minutes one way. But time spent at the barn on weekends made our hearts long for the country even more, despite the longer commute.

I knew it could be years or even decades before we built our new home in the country. Still, I began to leaf through house plan books and look at online home plans. When I didn't find anything that suited me, I began work on a design of my own – one that would work with our lifestyle and take advantage of the pastoral views. I didn't consider it work at all. It was a joy to plan and dream about the home God would give us one day.

Jimbo's nephew Randy or RJ as we call him, transferred to JBU in the fall of 2011. We enjoyed his visits for dinner and to catch up on his laundry. The fact that our home was only a mile from the school made it a convenient home-away-from-home for RJ. "Maybe we can build a home in the country after RJ graduates," Jimbo said. That was a far cry from his original plan to wait until retirement. Waiting until RJ graduated would put us in a new home sometime around the summer of 2014.

But keeping up two homes, one in town as well as the barn 30 minutes away, became increasingly difficult. There were two yards to mow, two tax bills to pay, gas spent running back and forth to keep an eye on things. It all began to add up. Finally, Jimbo's desire to settle down on one piece of property and our yearning to live in the country won out. Sometime in early February 2012 as we talked about our dream to live in the country, Jimbo turned to me and said, "Make it happen."

"What? You mean you're ready to build?" I asked.

"If we're going to make this move, let's go ahead and do it. Call the builder. Make it happen," he answered.

In February 2012 I got in touch with a local builder, Steve Bishop and we began to work together on a blue print for our new home. The process took longer than I expected as we kept finding ways to tweak my original plan and make it better. Each time we made a change I would hurry over to George and Carol's to show them the improvements we were making. They were just as excited as we were about our building a new home. And the fact we were ready to settle down on the land they had provided gave them some assurance we would not be leaving them. It was a dream-come-true for them and a promise fulfilled for me.

One afternoon I stopped by the Severns' to show them some changes I had made to our floor plan. George wasn't home, but Carol was eager to see the new developments. What she didn't understand from the blue print, she had me explain to her in detail. "Now how is this going to be laid out? And which direction will this window face? And how tall is this ceiling going to be?" she would ask.

After going over the plan thoroughly, we sat down for some coffee and a chat as we had so many times before. We began to talk about the events of the last four years – of Jimmy Ray's and my move to start Newsong. About his mysterious illness and his passing just as Newsong was starting to take off. About God's warning to me that Jimmy Ray would pass and how my life would reflect that of Ruth's in the Bible. And finally, we talked about how God had promised me a Boaz and the unlikely circumstances that had brought Jimbo and me back together again.

It was at this moment that Carol said something I will never forget. I will not forget it because they were words that could come only from a heart whose faith and confidence rested wholly in the sovereignty of

God. They came from a heart that was broken yet fully fixed on the goodness and wisdom of God her Father. She said, "You know, I'm selfish," and her voice began to break. Then she continued, "I wish you were still married to my son. But God is sovereign, and I believe it was meant for you and Jimbo to be together. Don't you?"

"Yes Carol, I do," I answered.

I was amazed by this woman's resolve. What could have shaken and destroyed her faith had only served to make it stronger. She was a tower of faith and an example of God's grace in the midst of tragic loss. And when God did not give her the future she had prayed for, she embraced the one he had granted.

In mid-May, 2012 Jimbo and I broke ground on our new home in the country. The weather was unusually hot and dry all summer. But the lack of rain, while a trial for the farmers, meant work on the house went on uninterrupted.

Jimbo and I spent more time than usual at the barn so we could keep an eye on construction. I remember one morning in particular. Excitement about the new house kept me from sleeping at times and I often rose at 3:30 or 4:00 in the morning. On this particular morning I had risen early with thoughts on how I might make the kitchen more functional. I turned on a dim light so as not to disturb Jimbo while I drew out the new plan.

As soon as it was daylight, I walked over to the new house, coffee in hand. The framing was about 80 percent complete and there were 2 x 4's still bracing the walls making it a bit difficult to walk through. But the exterior walls and windows were framed and the general shape of the house could easily be seen.

I stood in the middle of our newly-framed house and peered out what would be our new front windows. As I gazed out across the pasture and woods that lay beyond, I was reminded of the journey that had brought me here. I recalled those dark days when I wrestled with God's revelation to me that Jimmy Ray would die a young man. I recalled God's promises to me of land, of a home, and of a Boaz. I recalled our journey from Ellettsville to Newsong and God's great blessing on our work. I relived Jimmy Ray's sickness, his passing and the passing of the torch to not one but two of his spiritual sons. The torch would pass first to Pastor Roger Coleman who would eventually pass the torch to now *Pastor* CJ Brummett. Jimmy Ray would have been so very proud of both these young men, called and anointed by God to continue his legacy of ministry at Newsong.

I was amazed and overwhelmed as I recounted God's faithfulness, his blessing, and his love. I soon began to weep, unable to contain my gratitude and awe. "Thank you, God," I said through my tears. "I have done nothing to deserve this great blessing. But thank you."

It was only about 5:30 or 6:00 in the morning, but I had to share the moment with someone. I knew my dear friend Ruthie would be up at this hour so I called to share with her the gratitude and joy that had filled my heart.

"Ring...ring," I heard on the other end. I could hardly wait for her to answer.

"Hello," Ruthie said on the other end of the line.

"Hi, Ruthie. It's Lynn."

"Are you okay, honey?" she inquired, thinking something must be wrong for me to call so early.

"Yes, Ruthie. I'm fine." Then I began to explain. "I'm out here in the frame of my new house and I was just overwhelmed by God's blessing," I said as I began to weep again. "I have done nothing to deserve all of this, but I'm so thankful," I continued. "I just had to share it with someone."

Ruthie and I cried together as we talked about the journey, both the heartache and the faithfulness of God that had seen me through to this place of joy.

As the summer progressed, so did work on the house. And nearly every day George and Carol came up to check on the progress. They not only wanted to see how the house was shaping up, but George wanted to inspect the work to make sure it was being done properly. And when he made his inspections he was always happy to see the materials and workmanship more than met his approval.

Finally, on September 10th, 2012, just two years after Jimbo and I married, we moved into our new home in the country. But it is more than a house to me. It is the fulfillment of the promise of a faithful God.

Our new house sits right next door to the barn where Noah still resides. George and Carol are frequent and welcome guests at what we now refer to as "The Lodge." And on any given day you are likely to find Jimbo and me sitting hand in hand enjoying God's blessing from our new front porch.

AFTERWORD

Through this story of my journey I have endeavored to illustrate how dramatically our destinations can be impacted by the faintest whisper of our Heavenly Father. And it is my hope that you too will be inspired to listen for his voice as he calls to you.

I will admit that after Jimmy Ray's passing I experienced a time when I feared God's voice. I closed my ears and shielded my heart from what might be another devastating, life-altering message. But as I've had more time to reflect on the way God used the message to bring about light in the midst of darkness and to chart my path in the midst of uncertainty, I find myself opening my ears and my heart to his whisper once again.

"How," you may ask, "does one discern the whisper of God?" As I shared earlier, I often compare recognizing God's voice to the way one recognizes the voice of a close friend or relative. The more time you spend with someone, the more familiar his or her voice becomes. And after a time, if they call you on the telephone, they need only say, "Hello," before you know with whom you speak. You recognize their voice because you've heard it before. The ability to recognize God's whisper develops as your relationship with him develops.

But how does that relationship begin? It begins simply by answering his knock on the door of your heart. In Revelation 3:20 (NIV), Jesus says, **"Here I am! I stand at the door and knock. If anyone hears my voice and opens the door, I will come in…"** How does one go about answering that knock at the door? It's really very simple.

One first must recognize that from the start there is a door of separation that exists between God and us. This door of separation is created by a sinful nature that could only be atoned for by the sacrifice of God's sinless Son, Jesus Christ.

I John 1:9 (NIV) says, "If we confess our sins, he is faithful and just to forgive us our sins and to purify us from all unrighteousness." Once that barrier has been removed by our confession of sin and belief is placed in Jesus Christ, our communication lines to God are open.

If you're just beginning your journey, begin by reading God's Word, the Bible. God continually uses his Word to reveal himself and to communicate with us. I have found the New Living Translation Life Application Study Bible a good translation for daily Bible study. Or you may prefer The Message, a contemporary Bible written in today's American-English. If you're not sure where to start, you may find the first few books of the New Testament easiest to begin with, as well as the books of Psalms and Proverbs. It is then important to talk to God yourself. There is no special vocabulary or glossary of terms to learn. Just speak to him as you would to a trusted friend. That is how the journey begins.

CPSIA information can be obtained
at www.ICGtesting.com
Printed in the USA
LVOW10s0822171117

556676LV00017B/486/P